THIS IS HOW WE DO IT!

MAKING YOUR MARRIAGE A MASTERPEACE

by

MONTELL AND KRISTIN JORDAN

www.montellandkristin.com

THIS IS HOW WE DO IT!
Making Your Marriage A Masterpeace
by Montell & Kristin Jordan

Printed in the United States of America.

ISBN 9781498434751

www.xulonpress.com

THANK YOU!

We would like to thank: Kevin Kerr for cover design, Craig Obrist Photography, Mallory Cruz for editing, Dee Dee & Avery Nesbitt for our inspiration, the Bowies, Tyler Ward, Cathy Yardley, Dennis & Colleen Rouse and Victory World Church, our Moms, Dads, brothers and sisters and our family and friends. Every couple with faith in the covenant of marriage. Thanks to our children, Christopher, Catharine, Sydney, Skyler and Samantha. Thanks Megan Loving, Yolanda Garcia and family, and the Bryson family for audio recording, thanks Xulon Press for assisting the initial self publishing and creation of this project. Lastly, but most importantly we thank Jesus Christ for saving our souls and our marriage for all to see.

Table of Contents

An Introductory Love Letter

Greetings from Montell & Kristin Jordan-

Love placed a desire in our hearts to share our personal experiences with you in hopes that our lives will minister to young married couples and soon to be married couples with the intent to encourage, heal, strengthen and enlighten all to the many pitfalls that may arise in marriage. Although the journey may be challenging, everyone may reap the joy that comes along with fulfilling the commitment of marriage. Even if you have been married for some time and are reading this, we trust it will serve as confirmation to the truth of God's goodness in marriage -- *your marriage* -- or perhaps this serves as a refresher course of the promises God makes to those in matrimony and you just need a loving reminder.

We believe many people, both young and seasoned (a nice way of saying *old*), have negative perceptions of marriage and lack the desire to be married or stay married due to overwhelming examples of frustrated married folks who are worn down, struggling, visibly unhappy, unfaithful, unkempt, unsexed, complainers, whiners, and who present an image contrary to what God promises to be one of the most fulfilling experiences two people may ever experience together in a lifetime. We believe in this season God desires to raise up a standard of excited marrieds who are built up, flourishing, vibrantly happy, faithful, healthy, sexually fulfilled, edifiers and witnesses to God's promises being accurate and available to all who trust His word regarding marriage. We believe *you* are one of those couples He desires to use. We know this simply because if God is using our personal bullet-riddled, nuclear bomb-tested testimony, He can definitely use yours for His glory.

We have been married for 20+ years and have experienced many great achievements; but we easily have endured many more tremendous, even epic failures throughout our journey. Yet, through it all we remain dedicated to God and to each other, believing that just as we are the bride of Christ and that He will never leave us or forsake us, we esteem our unity to each other in that same manner. The beauty of our shared stories of success and failure is that through our transparency God will speak to you and prove that He is no respecter of persons, and as He has miraculously transformed our lives to remain happily and healthily married for 20 years, He will do the same for you. That is *good* news.

We often joke during our speaking engagements that when you *achieve* at something it is called "success," and when you *fail* at something it is called "experience." We then say, "And we have *a lot* of experience to share with you." Well, all kidding aside, there is an underlying element of truth that our marital flubs, errors, mistakes, failures and tragedies tend to outweigh our triumphs in regard to usefulness or relevance in the lives of others. Our failures, and ability through Christ to overcome them and allow them to become experience, are what is now considered to be valuable information for those actively observing our lives up close and personal (like our children, friends, family, church, co-workers) and those of you reading now.

So, why the title "Marriage Masterpeace?"

Life is filled with many moving parts and pieces, almost like a jigsaw puzzle that we are attempting daily to put together and complete. It is impossible to complete a puzzle when pieces are missing. We believe in our efforts to balance assembling the pieces of pursuing your purpose, challenges of church, relying on relationships, family and friends, calling and career, and ultimately being fulfilled, *marriage* is the "masterpiece" (as in the master – piece) that, when positioned in its proper place, shows how to *master peace*. Marriage completes the puzzle, and only then are we made complete. Society may argue that being self-sufficient and independent is a good thing, yet we are reminded that God *saw* that man was alone and He *said,* "It is not good." That thought is the foundation that will run through *Marriage Masterpeace*, and it was taken from a best seller known as the Bible.

To clear any confusion, we understand the world has attempted to define and redefine the institution of marriage. For all intents and purposes, and with no apologies made, we will subscribe to God's biblical definition of marriage according to scripture in Genesis two which is between a man and a woman, and choose not to add or take away anything from the word of God. We also are not offering refunds for this book, but we hope presenting this now will at least save you the trouble of reading our story only to find that we believe the word of God to be truth, regardless of what the word of man says that may effectively change laws that God already clearly defined. This is how we do it.

When Kristin is navigating through a story, you will see a [KJ] to reference she is narrating. Likewise, when Montell is sharing a detailed/longwinded story (although it probably won't be needed) an [MJ] will precede the text. Ultimately, an [MJ & KJ] will begin the places where we are both detailing our lives. We pray this will be a resource that both husbands and wives will examine together, as well as become a tool for singles who desire to one day be married to gain revelation and insight into the joys and gift of a godly, happy and satisfying marriage.

Marriage Masterpeace will hopefully reveal to you the faithful promises of God's word available to all willing to experience the freedom within the confines of Godly marriages shared through the scope of our personal journey. We know your story may be considerably different from ours; yet the Lord who is the same yesterday, today and forever presents truth that covers all our experiences and applies it to all who believe and love truth. Marriage is honorable in His sight. Marriage is referenced time and time again in the Bible (over 500 references), and many don't know that the word of God regarding marriage is applicable to both believers and non-believers. The word works; you just need to work the word. This is the direction we are heading.

It is our goal to provide you with some fundamental building blocks for a godly, healthy and happy marriage. We are going to share some life skills and hopefully help you establish some new mindsets. Hopefully throughout this journey we take together, you will have a clearer understanding of God's plan for your marriage.

We love God, His Son Jesus, The Holy Spirit, we love each other, and we heart *you* and the opportunity to sow our laughter, tears and life testimony into making your journey as wonderful as ours has been. God is love and walking in love means walking in God. We are walking in love down a road less traveled, in faith, to the destination of "happily married forever," and we pray you will take this path with us as we learn to *master peace.*

Montell & Kristin Jordan

CHAPTER 1

Boy Meets Girl

[KJ] We met in a rather interesting place; a place neither of us was supposed to be at that moment in time... or at least that is how it seemed. It was fall of 1991 in Los Angeles, CA. We met at a sorority ball, both attending at the invitation of friends. I could have never guessed that this day would change the course of the rest of my life moving forward. I would innocently go to a ball not knowing that my prince would await me. The absolute truth of the matter was I didn't even know I was a princess yet, and quite frankly if you asked him he would probably tell you I acted like a royal... well, let's just say "un-princess-like."

My best friend asked me to attend her sorority's ball and, despite my reluctance, I went. I entered the building and ran into an old college buddy from Sonoma State University. I greeted him and he introduced me to his brother, Montell. Now although the introduction was made, to be honest, I really didn't see him. At the time, I was in a place of disappointment and extremely self-absorbed. Guys had been a real let down and I was in serious "man-hater" mode. I had been stuck with the dinner bill one too many times. I was seeing guys through a filtered lens so even though I did meet him, I never actually saw him, if you understand what I'm saying.

Following introductions, my former college buddy asked my friend to dance and they both left me standing there with Montell. After several failed attempts to engage me in meaningful conversation, he suggested that we join our friends and everyone else on the dance floor. I turned him down several times, yet he was extremely persistent. After the ump-teenth request, I finally replied, "If I dance with you, will you leave me alone?" He smiled at me and agreed, and off to the dance floor we went.

Once on the dance floor, my friend and I were talking and laughing with each other, and apparently the guys were getting a little annoyed at our lack of attention. A few minutes later, the DJ put on an old dance classic that inspired the guys to try to get our attention by busting out some old-school dance moves. Montell is nearly seven-feet tall and these old school moves were larger than life. I'm not certain if you're familiar with the dance known as the "running man," but with his Goliath-like stature, you can imagine it was quite a sight to behold (just visualize all his appendages flailing out of control as if swatting at a swarm of angry bees and you'll get the idea). At that moment, I wasn't sure whether to be mortified or just laugh by the attention we were now attracting. I quickly grabbed his hand and whisked him off the dance floor. Earlier in the night, I had refused any inkling of a conversation, but following the horror that ensued I quickly changed my mind and said that we could talk if he promised not to dance anymore. I was suddenly overcome by nervous laughter and was in total disbelief at how he had commanded my attention. He refused to be ignored and he pursued me. Is this what being valued felt like? Still unsure of him, I began *the great inquisition*. Completely serious, I asked him, "Do you have a job?"

I'm sure this seemed like a strange question to ask within our first few moments of actual dialogue. However, many of the guys I previously dated were unemployed -- news I had to learn the hard way. A few years prior I was completing a dinner date and when the bill arrived, my date exclaimed, "You got me, right?" I wanted to scream, "Helicopter no! I most assuredly do not have you." Never desiring to experience the "you got me" episode again, my first question to every suitor became about his current employment. This may seem shallow, but even as a teen I was *not* interested in a man without a plan. Pay for me? No thanks. I was a product of a modern family that had seen divorce and remarriage several times. I was groomed by my mother to be self-sufficient and independent. I didn't need him to take care of me, but I certainly needed him to be able to cover himself.

He looked at me in utter amazement, astounded that I was so blunt and seemingly unaffected by his wit and charm. What I didn't know at the time was that he was the "King Kappa" in his fraternity and one of the most renowned fraternity brothers on the west coast. I would later find that it had been quite some time since a woman had given him the brush off, played hard to get, or *was* hard to get, so he was intrigued by the fact that I could absolutely care less who he was or from whence he came. After he explained that he was a Pepperdine graduate and worked at an advertising agency, I obliged when he asked for my number.

I really didn't think he'd call. I had never been on a date alone with anyone I hadn't known for at least three months, so I had no intention of actually going on a date with him. To my surprise, he called in two days, breaking the "wait at least three days before calling so you don't seem desperate" rule to suggest we go on a double date with his brother and my best friend. I was comforted by the idea that we would not be alone and were going out with our friends, so I agreed. Even prior to understanding, applying, or even being aware of the principles of courtship, we instinctively knew we would be safer with company. We decided to go out that weekend. Being girls who preferred to be in control, we arranged to drive and pick them up. We wanted to have a car just in case we felt uncomfortable or compromised in any way.

I often get asked if I believe in love at first sight. Perhaps not love at *first* sight, I say, but I do know it was the second time I saw this extraordinary specimen of a man that I fell in love. If I could have programmed theme music for that moment he stepped out onto the porch of his parents' house, dressed in an all-white track suit, Barry White's "Deeper and Deeper" would have been playing in the background. He looked like a million bucks and, in my mind, the light shown upon him and he was one of the handsomest men I had ever laid eyes on. My friend and I looked at each other in total disbelief; we most definitely didn't remember him being that handsome. Had I really "seen" him when we first met, I am certain it would have been love at first sight. One thing was for certain: the man that stood before me was a game changer. My friend looked at me in disbelief and blurted out, "Dag! I picked the wrong one!" We shared a big laugh yet, honestly, I am so glad she did. He got in the car and my friend and I quickly regained our composure. We drove to the movies to meet his brother and found there was nothing we really wanted to see. We rented a movie instead and headed towards a friend's apartment.

Once we arrived at this bachelor's college apartment, we coupled up and a conversation sparked between Montell and me. We never made it to watch the movie. Surprisingly, it didn't feel awkward at all. Here we were, two intelligent, charming, fascinating young people, attracted to each other. We began to talk and time was flying yet standing still at the same time. The conversation was insightful and incredibly deep. We were stunned at how we talked all night long and before we knew it, the sun was coming up. We talked about our biggest secrets, biggest fears, and most agonizing hurts. It was bizarre, yet so perfect. I had never felt like this in my life. We sat in the kitchen and watched the sunrise and I knew that this was something I had never experienced before. *He* was something I had never experienced before. That evening we were strangers and by morning, we were inseparable.

[MJ] With exception of the incorrect interpretation of my captivating dance moves, I would agree that our introduction happened just as my wife described. From my vantage point, I saw her before she entered the ball and my heart connected to her before she ever refused to acknowledge my existence. That very first night, we danced and I made her laugh. While it's true that it wasn't until the second date that *she* actually saw *me*, that first night I saw her. I *found* her. I had purposed in my heart that I was tired of dating and was ready to find the right one instead of just someone to pass the time. I had been in a few relationships before and found myself being the good guy who was capable of doing bad things. The word of God declares in Proverbs 18:22 that, *"He that finds a wife finds a good thing and obtains the favor of The Lord."* Even though we were both completely unaware of it, from the beginning we were a part of God's plan for each other.

[MJ & KJ] We would go on to be the absolute loves of each other's lives. Looking back, we both realize how perfectly ironic and purposeful our initial introduction was. While dating, we discovered that we knew all the same people and traveled in the same circles for years and yet somehow, we never met. We even interacted with family members (cousins) years prior. Until that appointed moment in time, we were not prepared for each other, so God literally blocked us from meeting or even knowing the other person existed. His timing was just right. What an awesome and perfect God we serve; one who is always on time and never late! Montell gets the girl of his dreams and Kristin gets the love of her life. Neither of us could be happier, nor ask for more. God gave us both His best.

Despite our current confidence in our marriage, the road has not always been an easy one. It is through our life circumstances, trials, tribulations, and triumphs that God has placed us -- two beautifully broken people -- together to shine a light on how you, too, can turn your marriage into a "master-peace." God has taken two wildly imperfect people and created an example of what only He can do. It is our prayer that as we share our lives with you and reveal some of the wisdom He has given us that you will also walk in freedom, joy, love and peace.

As our lives literally become an open book, it is our desire for you to experience our testimony. We ask that you prayerfully reflect on the similarities and differences to your own personal journey so you may learn some of the key steps that have made our marriage a master peace!

We believe the word *master* means to be eminently skilled.

We believe the word *peace* means to free your mind from annoyances, distractions, anxieties, and obsessions and to be in a mutual state of harmony.

We share our story with the desire to equip you to be eminently skilled in freeing your mind and creating a place or state of harmony in your marriage. We will walk you through some of the tools and information that has aided us in making these last two decades a piece of Heaven on earth.

Take a moment to reflect on the first time you actually "saw" your spouse for the first time. If it is a good memory, rekindle and embrace that moment. Share the experience with your loved one.

CHAPTER 2

God's Blueprint

[MJ & KJ] Growing up, neither one of us had a good example of marriage modeled for us. Combine that with what we see on television, reality shows, film, social media and sometimes even through our personal friends and family, and we had no idea what marriage was supposed to look like. We, just like modern society, had a distorted view of what marriage was supposed to look like. Fortunately, God provides a blueprint on how to have a successful marriage, and by following this blueprint, we can avoid many of the pitfalls that are being modeled all around us.

We truly believe God has made available the blueprint for a successful marriage. All people are created and designed differently, and every marriage will have its own unique set of challenges; however, God's blueprint can apply to everyone. A blueprint is simply a template that allows something to be created with ease by providing useful, previously documented directions. Having a template or design makes it easier to construct or build something.

For example, someone may have an idea for designing a dress. One can try and create it from their thoughts of what they perceive a dress to look like or they can create it from a pattern that someone else has already put in the time to construct. Someone might have a desire to build a shed and even have all the tools required to get the job done, but without the knowledge on how to build it, they're lost. In both of these instances, having a simple set of instructions can greatly help the creator to reach the desired goal. The pattern makes the process less painful as it provides direction, simplicity and efficiency to achieve the desired result. This blueprint does not simplify the actual building process, but rather assists in the process by providing a target or end result. It also provides instruction of which tools are to be used when and where.

Like the architect He is, God allowed us to experience many difficult things throughout our marriage so that we could construct a workable pattern for others to build upon. Now, we can provide what the end result can look like: a happy, healthy and eternal marriage. God knows we are different. After all, He created us that way. Because each person is different, He allows us all the ability to modify our blueprint through personal choice to ultimately build the marriage of our dreams. Despite how difficult it may become, we must stay true to the original plan, regardless of the changes and/or additions that come our way.

It's no surprise that lots of trial and error must take place to construct a template that will provide the easiest way to duplicate success. It has been said that a wise person learns from the mistakes of others, while a foolish person chooses to learn from his own. For those seeking to be wise, we have documented our foolish marital expenditures for the sake of the blueprint. We often say that when you achieve at something, it is called "success," and when you epically fail at something, it is often called "experience." It is this compilation of experiences that ultimately becomes the blueprint. Success often bears fruit that others can see, while experience is just a fancy way of saying we have learned what not to do. Fortunately for you, we are versed with both the successes and experiences of over 20 years. The cool thing about having a usable set of instructions is that anyone can follow the blueprint as long as they have the right tools and are committed to following the blueprint.

Believe it or not, there was a time when upholding marital principles and values was esteemed as the line not to be crossed. However, in the world we live in now, marriage is not viewed the same as it was 50, 20 or even five years ago and our fundamental morals continue to change as society changes. Unfortunately, we have allowed our society, the government and even our own carnal desires to devalue the meaning of the family building block we call *marriage*. The waves of change have come crashing down on our values, erasing whatever trace of a moral line remained.

24 "Anyone who listens to my teaching and follows it is wise, like a person who builds a house on solid rock. 25 Though the rain comes in torrents and the flood-waters rise and the winds beat against that house, it won't collapse because it is built on bedrock. 26 But anyone who hears my teaching and doesn't obey it is foolish, like a person who builds a house on sand. 27 When the rains and floods come and the winds beat against that house, it will collapse with a mighty crash." Matthew 7:24-27 (NLT)

As we are writing, our nation has currently legalized gay marriage in 37 states, and more are certain to follow. What was once considered "normal" by definition is no longer normal. Lovingly, we look to the word of God and the example of Jesus to determine the blueprint provided for a healthy, Godly covenant between a man and woman. With no disrespect to any other form of redefined marriage, civil union, new interpretation or legal addendums, it is our belief that God's plan works best in the confines of the original pieces He designed the blueprint with and for: husband and wife. As the old hymn sings, "On Christ the solid rock I stand; all other ground is sinking sand."

We began asking the Lord to break our hearts for what breaks His and we became instantly overwhelmed with the fact that marriages are in a state of emergency! According to 2014 census bureau statistics provided from www.census.gov, 50% of all marriages end in divorce. That is staggering, but maybe even more shocking is that this statistic is exactly the same amongst Christians and non-Christians.[1] Whether you are in church or not, the statistics remain the same. We should be alarmed that half of all marriages will end in divorce, regardless of their spirituality. The census also informs that the current average life span of a marriage is now only 8 years. Many of us have shoes and purses older than that! It becomes painfully obvious that although many are saying, "I do," they are really saying, "I do...until I don't." Instead of entering into marriage with an exit strategy, we suggest having an *eternal* strategy.

Needless to say, we are at a tipping point. Half of all marriages are ending in divorce and many singles are considering never getting married at all. Who can blame them? The examples they witness often lead them to say, "Why bother? If more marriages fail than succeed, why should I even bother to get married? Perhaps I'm better off being alone."

Here's food for thought:

> *12 A person standing alone can be attacked and defeated, but two can stand back-to-back and conquer. Three are even better, for a triple-braided cord is not easily broken. Ecclesiastes 4:12 (NLT)*

Early in creation, The Lord saw Adam alone in the garden and said, "It is *not* good that man should be alone," (Genesis 2:18, emphasis added). Even if we are single or alone, *loneliness* is *not* desired for any of us as it leaves us open to potential misery and bondage like you can't even imagine. Although not everyone will experience the joys of marriage in their lifetime, singles need to know the difference between being secluded and being isolated. One can have community and relationships with family and friends and the Father in seclusion, but isolation allows the enemy the opportunity to take you out... and not in a good way. The Lord seeks to draw near to us in seclusion; the enemy seeks to steal, kill and destroy us when isolated.

These divorce statistics really turned on the light to just how serious this situation is. When the ultimate promise between husband and wife -- the covenant of marriage -- is discarded, devalued and made so matter-of-fact, it causes a paradigm shift. This shift affects the way we view marriage and how we value the importance of it in our lives. We begin to think of it as disposable. When adversities and trials come, instead of making the effort to work things out, we begin looking for a way out. Rather than seeking a solution, we begin looking for an exit strategy, causing us to run *from* God rather than *to* God. We can see why the outlook of the current and next generation is jaded when it comes to marriage. However, we do want you to see that the father of lies is behind these attempts to redefine marriage. As soon as we begin to entertain these lies, poisonous thoughts begin to invade our relationships and its venom slowly begins to cause paralysis in our communication, commitment to each other and the sacred covenant made between God and our spouse.

These toxic thoughts in marriage are extremely dangerous. They don't always come all at once but like a painful paralysis, it sometimes progresses gradually and slowly over time. Symptoms often begin to reveal themselves differently. For some, it may come in the form of living with offense, busyness, stress from lack or abundance of finances, addiction to pornography (for both males and females), lack of communication leading to withholding intimacy, priorities being out of alignment, disappointments, depression and oppression, experiencing tragedy and a multitude of additional things. Every one of these symptoms has the potential to bring separation, discord and divorce from the most important covenant we will ever make with another human. Outside of the personal covenant we make regarding our salvation in Christ, this is the most important covenant we make in our lifetime.

Marriage is a precious thing in the sight of God. If that were not the case, He would not have spoken that "it was not good for man to be alone" (Genesis 2:18) or "he that finds a wife finds a good thing and obtains favor from The Lord," (Proverbs 18:22.). He even refers to His chosen people, the church, as His "bride." Scripture has numerous accounts of Christ likening marriage to the relationship He longs to have with us. If it is important to Him, it should be important to us.

The Merriam-Webster Dictionary provides multiple definitions that describe *favor* as *"finding preferential treatment and to be held in high regard or approval over another."*[2] If we are going to find favor with anyone, surely He's the one from whom we want to obtain it. An interesting note is that the biblical law promising favor works regardless of whether or not you are a Christian. If you look at that proverbial scripture, it does not say, "If you are a Christian and you find a wife, then you obtain favor from the Lord." God loves and honors marriage so much that *the law works no matter who is working it.* It's just like gravity. If you go up to the top of a 10-story building believing the laws of gravity don't apply to you and jump off the roof, you *will* be quickly and painfully be reminded that the laws of gravity *do* indeed apply to *everyone.* We must be aware of those limitations as that boundary is set in place for our own good. The promise of favor from marriage is a law that applies no matter who applies it. Without adding to or taking anything away from God's word, *"he* that finds a *wife"* applies to *any* he that finds a wife.

* Sidebar: Notice the scripture (blueprint) doesn't say:

- She that finds a husband.

- He that finds a husband.

- She that finds a wife.

[KJ] In my family, I saw a lot of unhealthy marriage patterns that left me professing that I never wanted to be married. If what I had seen was an accurate reflection of marriage, I simply wanted no part of it. By the time I was eighteen years old, both of my parents had been married six times and divorced five times, each to different people. Divorce became a way of life, a blueprint, in my childhood. I learned to cope with things by closing chapters in my mind as if they were chapters in a book so I could compartmentalize and deal with them one by one (or not deal with them at all). I saw and experienced abandonment, rejection, fear, sexual, physical and mental abuse and drug and alcohol addiction, just to name a few. This was a lot for a kid to process, but what it did was establish in me what I did not want in my life moving forward. I absorbed these experiences and allowed them to become my blueprint of what not to do. I have seen the results of marital dysfunction and divorce up close and personal and the effects it takes on the people involved. I assure you, there is nothing good that comes out of it. Nothing.

[MJ] I grew up in a family that experienced divorce in a completely different way. After 25 years of a healthy marriage, at least from a child's eyes, I watched my family become completely disenfranchised by an unexpected divorce. The Jordan household that was once a neighborhood and church safe haven would eventually dismantle, along with much of the closeness shared between my three siblings and myself. I tried to sort out my role and contribution to the divorce. I sought to find the ways that I was personally responsible for my parents' separation and made sure to take a nice portion of guilt with me as I left college and headed into the real world.

The guilt I experienced rooted itself in my request for financial assistance to attend college and how that may have contributed to our family's economic distress. It was also once alluded to that due to my mom's young motherhood (having me 3 days prior to her 18th birthday), she missed much of her childhood. Perhaps becoming a parent at a young age caused her to now attempt to regain her lost youth apart from my father and the confines of her marriage. Either way, I found myself seeking to shoulder the responsibility of my parents' separation.

I knew other kids who had grown up in broken homes and was sympathetic to their plight, but now it was me. It was as if my entire family was actually getting divorced, not just my parents. Many years later Kristin and I were receiving marital counseling for our own relationship and during an exercise, we analyzed my lineage and discovered a history of repetitive broken relationships, infidelities, children outside of marriage, family secrets and unhealthy patterns that would lend to my own destructive thoughts about what a marriage looked like.

[MJ & KJ] Needless to say, when we first got together there were *not* many healthy foundations and blueprints to reference how to make a marriage work. The only marriage relationship that stood out to us as a blueprint was that of Kristin's grandparents, married for 54+ years. Grandpa and Grandma Newbould were rooted and grounded in the Lord and had the longest, most successful marriage we knew of at the time. Naturally, when we decided marriage might be the road we were headed down, we decided to seek their advice to see what would lie ahead. A pastor friend, Johnson Bowie, once spoke in a message, "If you wanna know what lay down the road ahead, ask someone who is on the way back." We wanted to know how you know when someone is *the one* and how do you know it will last forever? We asked them and they both just looked at each other and then to us, smiled, and said, "You just know."

Honestly, we were less than thrilled with their answer. Surely the long-awaited and highly-anticipated answer to one of life's greatest marital mysteries was more than, "you just know." They shared many things with us, but our most prized take away from that conversation became our marriage mantra: *rocking chairs and beyond*. This is the foundation or blueprint that we built our marriage upon. It was solid advice through biblical instruction (building our marriage on the rock, not on sand), seeking Godly mentors and accountability (there is safety in a multitude of wise counsel), and not just hearing the word of God but applying it so He would ultimately get the glory from our lives unified in marriage. We believe it is this foundation that has been the blueprint of turning our marriage into a *masterpeace*.

Please note that these practices did not keep us from experiencing devastating difficulties in our marriage, yet they would provide the means to overcome. Know that in the face of the obstacles we encountered, we had the instructions of what to do in case of emergency. Trust us, emergencies did come; the blueprint simply advised us how to endure the storm and become overcomers.

What to do: Take a few moments and reflect and discuss what your current blueprint looks like. Even if you weren't aware that you were working from one, hopefully you are able to identify the templates, measurements and tools that have crafted your marriage into its current state. Perhaps even write down some of the vows made, good or bad, that are now playing themselves out currently in marriage. Identify what the blueprint currently looks like, solid or shaky. After individually writing these, share them with your spouse. No solutions are needed yet; just share.

After reading this chapter, many may need an extreme marriage makeover. If that's you, don't worry. In the next chapter, we are going to renovate and will begin by building a sound foundation on solid ground.

CHAPTER 3

First Things First

[MJ & KJ] In order for our marriage to be in the perfect will of God, we must learn how to put things in proper order. When our life gets out of order or we place something less important over something more important, our lives get out of alignment and dysfunction arrives on our doorstep. We must get our priorities straight and keep them that way in order for everything to function decently and in order. Whenever we sense chaos or a strenuous pull on our lives, we have to make sure our priorities are in alignment with God's will for our lives. The brother of Jesus writes in James 3:16, *for where you have envy and selfish ambition, there you find disorder and every evil practice*. A marriage being built from a solid blueprint requires that we put things in place and in the proper order. Fortunately, the Bible gives us a great template to use when organizing our list of priorities:

1. God (personal relationship)

2. Spouse

3. Children

4. Church / Ministry (serving or corporate gathering)

5. Extended Family and special friends

6. Work or Career

7. Hobbies, Sports, and Other Interests

We are in agreement with most Christian marriage counselors who agree with this list of priorities. Anthony and Phyllis Breech also detail this list, in *Married Forever*, a ministry resource available at www.victoryatl.com from Victory World Church.

1. God

[MJ & KJ] The first thing on the list is our personal relationship with God. This is the most important relationship and the first building block of our blueprint. Getting this means we get everything. The Bible says we are to love the Lord with our whole heart, love Him with all that's within us and with all we've got! (Deut. 6:5) There is no thing and no one that should be placed or prioritized above our personal relationship with God. It is very important to keep our God relationship prioritized over our spouse, children, ministry, job or whatever vies for our affections. Not doing so puts the people and things we love in jeopardy.

[KJ] My youngest son, Skyler, was about seven years old when he randomly asked me who I loved the most. I thought it was an odd question, but I knew that this was a critical teaching moment and that my answer could shape his future. I asked him, "What do you mean, baby?"

He said, "Do you love me more than God?" I paused for a second and reminded him of a scripture we had read a few weeks prior in *The Action Bible: God's Redemptive Story by* Sergio Cariello[3]. *"And you shall love The Lord your God with all your heart, with all your soul, with all your mind and with all your strength. This is the first commandment," Mark 12:30 (NKJV).* I asked if he remembered that, and he nodded.

I said, "Baby, there is no one I love more than God and there is no one you should love more than God... even Mommy." His eyes got real big, but I assured him that this was pleasing to God and that putting God first would protect our whole family. He thought about it for a second and then he said, "I get that, Mommy, and I do love God the most." He then told me not to worry because I was next (over Daddy). In such an innocent question from my son, I was able to teach him a principle that would change his life. Anything you put before God is an *idol* and will most assuredly be moved. We serve a jealous God and He does not want to share our first affections with anything or anyone else.

[MJ] Early on in our marriage, Kristin and I were both extremely career driven. We were both Christians and loved the Lord. We even tithed regularly. However, neither of us really ever thought that God or each other should be made priority over our successful careers. Ultimately, our career aspirations and achievements began to define us more than who we were in Christ. This would cause tremendous tension in our marriage as we placed more value on our jobs than on each other, resulting in several years of difficulty in every area imaginable. Even greater than this, our closeness and ability to hear from God diminished and we often found ourselves without spiritual guidance in a music world where we desperately needed our steps ordered. Our intimacy suffered, our financial decisions were haphazard and our church life waned as we endeavored to do it "our way." People who simply watched us from afar had no idea we were married. Even those close to us saw us as a successful, Godly couple. No one could see the turmoil behind the scenes.

It took years to understand that my wife had difficulty submitting to someone who was not first submitted to God. When sin first happened in the Garden of Eden, God went looking for Adam (the head of the house), even though Eve took the first bite. Every aspect of my personal life was in chaos until I came into alignment as the head of my family and allowed myself to be totally submitted to Jesus. The same way God came looking for Adam, he came looking for me, ready to hold me accountable for the wife and gifts He had entrusted to me. I encourage every man to know that a Godly woman loves to submit to a man who is submitted to God.

I experienced this in my own marriage and know this to be true. When a man is completely submitted to God, he doesn't have to try and change his wife; God does the refining and transformation to redesign the woman of our dreams.

2. Spouse

[MJ & KJ] The priority that should be next in our lives after God is **our spouse**. Marriage is a covenant relationship between three people: God, you and your spouse. There is no other earthly relationship that should take precedence over our marriage. The Bible instructs in Genesis 2:24 for us to leave our mother and father and cleave (cling) to our spouse. Blessing and protection are our promised rewards when we are obedient to the priorities God has laid before us. Let this promise be activated in our marriages. To place this relationship in any other order is disobedience to God and can block us from receiving favor and blessing.

We have often been in impromptu counseling sessions and have heard guys say, "I will do anything for my daughter. She comes first." Or we will hear a woman say, "I love him, but my independence is important to me." These statements might seem harmless, but to us they are evidence that the areas of difficulty in the marriage or relationship are directly related to first things not being first. What wife wants to be placed behind a child? What husband wants to rank behind a job? We have also spoken with many blended families and found this to be a common theme or point of contention.

As each parent is bringing children from a previous relationship or marriage into the current marriage, loyalty to their own children over their spouse is a constant source of division within the marriage.

We love our children to life, all five of them. However, none of them come before our marriage. They all understand trying to put mom and dad at odds is a no-no. This is a learned behavior that they do not get through osmosis, but through training from Godly parents. It is our job to let them know what the home structure will look like according to God's word. Homes where the children are allowed to dictate the order of the house will most likely result in a restless place with no peace. Husbands and wives become adversaries instead of advocates for each other while the kids become referees, determining family structure and policy. This is not God's design. He designed the man to be submitted to the Lord, the wife to be submitted to her husband as unto the Lord, and the children to be submitted to their parents. By implementing this into our kids, we set them up to not only honor us as parents, but they also become beneficiaries of the promise of long life the Bible promises to them in Exodus 20:12: *"Honor your father and mother. Then you will live a long, full life in the land the Lord your God is giving you," (NLT).*

Following our personal relationship to God, our commitment to our spouse is the most vital relationship we can nurture here on the Earth. God desires to be first, and then created us to be even closer to Him through relationship with our spouse.

We often reflect on how Adam appeared to have the perfect life. He had a home, a job, access to anything he wanted and a personal one-on-one relationship with the Father in Heaven. They were so close that God would walk beside him in the garden in the cool of the day. God created all these things and saw it was good. Adam had all access to creation and God himself yet the word instructs, *"Then the Lord God said, 'It is not good for the man to be alone. I will make a helper who is just right for him,'" Genesis 2:18 (NLT).*

Have you ever wondered why God would say that? After all, Adam was not alone. He had God right there with him. Wouldn't God be just right for him? We believe that even as close as God was to Adam, He desired to be even *closer.*

When Adam was having a bad day at the office and needed a shoulder to cry on, he could not lean on God's shoulder in Heaven, so God created Eve to provide that shoulder. When God desired to comfort Adam and hold his hand, a gigantic hand didn't come from the heavens to hold Adam's; yet the soft tender hand of Eve, his spouse, was prepared for him and made readily available to provide the touch from God. When God desired to look into Adam's eyes, face to face, a giant face didn't come from the sky to see Adam; yet Eve, his spouse, was designed to lovingly look into his eyes and into his soul to provide the tenderness and loving approval that God Himself seeks to show us all. Our spouses become the hands, shoulders, eyes and heart of God. God did not visibly walk beside Adam. After all, He is God. However, Eve could. Our spouses have that same capability.

Adam was also there for Eve. As she was speaking about the half-off fig leaf sale in the garden consignment store, God's ear didn't miraculously fall from the sky to lend an ear. However, Adam was there to listen (or at least nod approvingly as though he were listening). When God desired to pull Eve close and hold her in His arms, enormous holy arms did not break through the clouds to hold and console her. Instead, it was Adam whose arms embraced her. When Eve ate of the forbidden fruit, could it be that Adam joined her in disobeying God because the aftermath of what was to come from her sin may have resulted in Adam being alone again, apart from the closest thing he had to God Himself here on Earth... Eve? He, too, ate of the fruit and joined her in receiving punishment. What a love story!

God created us and draws us closer to Himself through our spouses. When we function as His hands and feet to serve our spouses, as His heart to love our spouses and as His eyes to see our spouses, we are fulfilling His will and walking in the blueprint created for one of the greatest blessings God created for us through marriage. Following our personal relationship to God, there is no other relationship God honors more than the one that exists between a husband and wife.

3. Children

[MJ & KJ] The next priority is our children. We must learn where to prioritize our efforts, energy and time on our children, as they are our inheritance. After you and your spouse are no longer here, they are the legacy that will live on. How we prioritize and honor them will be a direct representation of what kind of legacy we leave.

[KJ] I've heard parents say, "Parenting is difficult because kids don't come with instruction manuals." Actually, this isn't true. Our instruction manual is the Bible and our example of a loving father is demonstrated by our Heavenly Father. The sad truth is most parents, non-believing and Christian alike, have never read the Bible cover to cover and therefore lack the tools needed to build a strong parenting foundation. It's impossible to be a confident parent without accurate information from the ultimate source and expert in parenting -- God. We can never truly know who we really are until we go to the original manufacturer and designer to see why we were made.

The more we become like our Heavenly Father and live the principles Jesus laid before us, the more capable and equipped parents we become. Being more like our Dad means we sacrifice, we love unconditionally, we chase after our children even when they are disobedient, we correct them, we show kindness and we believe in them. Christ's ultimate example has been modeled for us; it requires us to die to our own flesh in order to become the parents God desires us to be. One of the most common errors we see is parents loving their kids so much they elevate them over their relationship with God and their spouse. Both actions are incredibly dangerous. We jeopardize our marriages and potentially the lives of those we love when we exalt them over God and our matrimony.

[MJ] We all love our children, so it's understandable how they can become a priority in our lives. This is a good thing! They just shouldn't come before our personal relationship with the Lord and commitment to our spouse. Those first two relationships, when modeled correctly, become the solid foundation or blueprint for the children we love so dearly to work from and work towards as they walk their personal growth journeys. When we execute this properly, we are in God's will and word that admonishes us to *"Train up a child in the way he should go: and when he is old, he will not depart from it." (Proverbs 22:6, KJV).* Kristin and I have found that whenever chaos or disruption occurs within our daily family lives, reviewing this order often reveals where the issue lies.

I have been guilty of allowing all sorts of tasks, responsibilities and personal recreations to become a hazard to this order. My wife will sometimes have to remind me, "Babe, I love how you are leading and ministering to people, but our kids are missing you." I have learned a sobering reality: *How can a man take care of God's house and not take care of his own?* It is not God's desire or design for us to serve in ministry at the neglect of ministering in our own homes first. As parents, we are to be the priests in our homes, creating and sustaining an atmosphere of peace and worship where our children can excel. It is this overflow that should spill over into our house of worship, the church.

4. Church

[MJ & KJ] Our fourth priority is church, which includes ministry or assembly with a local body of believers. We often hear the phrase, "I don't have to go to church to have a relationship with God." We have found that most of the time, these "couch Christians" are either burnt out or have deep wounds from previous church hurts. Contrary to the idea that church involvement is optional, Hebrews 10:25 reminds us to not forsake the assembly of the saints so that we can *encourage*, *warn*, and *urge* each other on in the faith. Let's review these three reminders.

Encourage: We highly advise being a part of a small group, Bible study or some form of ministry to help keep perspective and provide access to accountability. God lifts us up and we are encouraged through others as the local body of believers. When functioning according to His will, we become the hands and feet of Jesus. Being unsatisfied with church is not an excuse to just sit back and watch, but instead a greater reason to become the love of Christ that we don't feel we are seeing.

Warn: "*A person standing alone can easily be attacked and defeated but two can stand back to back and conquer!*" *(Ecclesiastes 4:12, NLT).* We are much stronger when we are connected to the body of Christ and this helps us to continue to fight the good fight even when we feel isolated and alone. As we press forward, keeping our eyes to mountainous blessings the Lord has prepared for us, we need a body of believers to help "watch our back," as we used to say back in the old neighborhood. None of us are capable of moving forward while looking behind us.

Urge: Being around other believers challenges us to rise to greater heights and dive into deeper depths of our faith. Gym workouts with a personal trainer often produce greater results because they are positioned to push us beyond that which we believe we are capable of accomplishing. Likeminded believers provide that same atmosphere. Being in a community of strong, faith-filled believers can promote spiritual maturity that may not be attainable by spiritually "working out" alone.

[KJ] Here is another important reminder to all pastors, ministers, lay leaders and those who serve in church (warning: This may hurt). Working and serving at the church should never become more important than our direct relationship with the Lord, our spouse or our children, in that order. In other words, our personal relationship with God and our service to the church are *not* the same. *Don't sacrifice your children upon the altar of ministry!* Even working for a church does not replace our personal relationship with God, our commitment to our spouse or our dedication to our kids. As my wise husband always says: If that hurt and you can't say "Amen," just say "Ouch!"

[MJ] I often think back to a spiritual mentor of mine who was a catalyst for me leaving my music career and entering into full-time ministry. He had been in music ministry for over 20 years and was one of the most highly accomplished, gifted and anointed musicians I have ever known. Unfortunately, through his many years of service in ministry, the act of serving somehow began to replace his actual relationship with Jesus. Worship went from relationship to routine. As years went by, his gift carried him through the motions -- all technically correct -- that a worship service required, yet passion and direct relationship with Jesus were absent. This began to spill over into his home, his marriage and even those serving under him in ministry. When hearing sermons spoken on the weekends, he would initially listen, but then respond that he had heard them all before. The very principles presented in the message were not applied to, nor present in, his life. Over the years, his service *to* the Lord replaced his relationship *with* the Lord.

Please understand, Jesus doesn't want our works; He desires our hearts. Many people who love God make the mistake of thinking that being in the church means the church is in us. This man placed his ministry above his children, his wife and most importantly, his connection to the very One he was so diligently serving. As his spiritual life flat-lined, his marriage suffered and his kids were missing their dad. It wasn't until being counseled and made aware of this exchange that he was able to move forward towards reigniting his personal relationship with Jesus, his wife and his children. In a difficult but admirable leap of faith, he stepped away from ministry to step back towards focusing on his relationship with the Lord.

After these issues were addressed and his life began to realign with God's designed order, he was able to once again begin using his gifts to serve in ministry. This time, he had a renewed passion to a God who was once again alive within him. Upon speaking with him last, his marriage to his wife had regained its rightful place over his marriage to ministry, which spilled the blessing down over his children, transforming his entire home. Now his leadership in his home is more readily available to be used in the church.

God first, spouse second, children third, and church fourth.

5. Family and Friends

[MJ & KJ] The fifth priority is our extended family and friends. This is one of the priorities that is most often out of alignment, especially in newly married couples. It is imperative that our parents, siblings and friends all be strategically placed within our list of priorities. As a side note, just because they are your relatives doesn't make them your family. We don't get to choose our relatives but we *do* get to choose our family! Sometimes that includes your relatives and sometimes it does not. Families are the people *you choose* to do life with outside of your spouse and children. Proverbs 18:24 says *that some friends don't help but a true friend is closer than your own family*. There's nothing wrong with spending time with your relatives, as long as it is within the guidelines of your priorities.

Just as a chiropractor knows the spine and which adjustments are necessary to relieve pressure and pain and restore normalcy and functionality to our bodies, we must make adjustments and use that same chiropractic technique in the spirit. When our family or friends convince us that we are in church too much and then we find ourselves straying from ministry, chances are the family and friend vertebrae is shifted and placed above the church verte-brae. We will therefore feel the tension, guilt and pressure of being drawn from the ministry just as a muscle would feel when strained or disjointed from its proper position.

The desires of even our very own parents (or "Mama and 'Nem" as we said in the neighborhood) can find us compromising our faith, marriage, children and ministry when their will is imposed above the order God has given us. Family and friends will question our dedication in tithing, our commitment of time spent serving in ministry, and even cause us to question our own faith when diffi-culties arise in our lives. If family and friends are a higher priority within the blueprint structure, we will surely succumb to their thoughts over God's plan and we will most certainly find ourselves in need of another chiropractic adjustment.

[KJ] I can remember a time when my friends would call me to go hang out at the mall or go see a movie. This typically would be okay when my husband was not in town; however, once he came back into town my automatic answer should have been, "I am unavailable." Truthfully, early on in our marriage I did not spend time doing the things I should have and I was totally out of order by not telling my friends, "We will have to do it another time," and making my husband my priority. God believes in order. He gave strict instructions and dimensions on how to build an ark, how the priests were to build a tabernacle, how they were to worship in it, and who was ordained to do it. I submit that a God committed to so much detail would also require some guidelines for us to provide a stable foundation in something He finds as important as marriage.

6. Career

The sixth and probably the most misplaced priority of all would be our career, work or job. Many workaholics and overachievers make the classic mistake of making this top priority, more important than anything else on the blueprint list.

[KJ] Have you ever heard someone say they can't go to church because they work on Sunday? Perhaps this is you. This is someone who has his or her priorities out of alignment. "I can't go to my son's football game this Saturday, I've got to work." (career vs. children)

Or maybe, "I would love to take you for our anniversary dinner but I have a conference. I've got to make money to provide for us, right?" (career vs. spouse)

"I would love to be able to get up and pray, but I have to be into work too early this morning." (career vs. God)

Be very cautious to not make work or a job a higher-ranking priority than where it should be. Doing so will may very well be putting that job and family in harm's way. Don't get me wrong, the Lord wants us to work, just not to the detriment of His relationship with us, our spouse, our children (if we have them) and our church and extended family. Ultimately, God is our provider, not us. Would the Lord really give us a job that would draw us away from Him? Would He bless us with something that could keep us away from serving Him? Often *we* pursue a job and *we* take a position and *we* don't consult Him for His opinion or His will and then *we* ask God to bless what *we* chose. Sometimes God is actually blessing us by saying no. There are occasions when He will give us what He knows we don't need simply because He loves us and we asked for it. We later realize that it wasn't what *we* needed after all and now we must deal with the consequences of our choices.

How often have you heard someone at the end of their life say that they wish they had spent more time at work, crunching numbers? Probably never. Most often the regret comes from missed family time, not taking vacations, skipping life events (games, graduations), neglecting to create lifetime memories and deferring special moments with a spouse for a few more hours on the job.

Unfortunately, we spend far more time with the gift of a job than the Gift-Giver of our job. Often, when the occupation has fulfilled its purpose, we realize we don't know Jesus as intimately as we could have.

[MJ] Kristin and I have hundreds of examples of how this one priority being out of place may cause the entire house of cards to come crashing down. More than the other priorities, this one has the ability to cause the most damage as finance is a key motivator and contender for our affections and attention. Matthew 6:21 says, "For where your treasure is, there your heart will be also." Unfortunately, many of us have hearts that are striving for success and focused on achievement, attempting to take the place of God as provider.

I was speaking at our satellite campus one Sunday morning when an extremely distraught couple approached my wife and me during the altar call. They were a blended family and were placing their individual children's needs above each other, causing chaos in their marriage to the point where they had separated and were now considering divorce. In addition, the wife also had an occupation that kept her out extremely late and required her to work odd hours on a regular basis. Despite the demanding schedule, she chose to climb the corporate ladder, often leaving behind her husband and children. This made it even more difficult to work on the marriage, parenting and building of their family. They had their first priority of personal relationship with Jesus in order, yet those other elements presented insurmountable difficulties to overcome. Kristin and I spoke with them regarding God's order and challenged them to give it a test run before pulling the plug. We shared the principle of first things first with them and before they left, they agreed to try the blueprint. Nearly seven weeks later, they approached us following a service, looking like completely different people.

They stood before the altar and confirmed that God is faithful. With teary eyes and huge smiles, they began to explain how once they had shifted their priorities, significant change began immediately. Now, their intimacy and relationship to each other dramatically shifted as they placed each other above their children. Also, the wife began praying for a new job that would not require such long and difficult hours. Taking a leap of faith, she resigned and sent out a résumé. Within 1 week, she got a direct call, not from human resources but from the owner of a facility in her profession who asked her what she was doing *that day*. An interview was set up for the following day and she was offered a great position. She is now continuing on her career path but this time, her focus on her career is in its proper place behind honoring God, her husband, her children and the ministry. We can never know how these stories end, yet we trust God will remain faithful in response to our faithfulness to Him.

7. Personal Interests

The last priority on the list is our personal interests, hobbies, sports and other forms of entertainment.

[KJ] Perhaps your husband likes to play golf, is a gamer or (like my husband) becomes immersed in the annual world of fantasy football. While there is a place in our life for these things, it comes after the other priorities are secured and taken care of. For years, Montell was involved in several online virtual leagues, all at once. For me, this stirred up some painful memories.

As a child, my dad was a cameraman who often filmed for the NFL and my mom was completely immersed in the football world, so much so that I would often become a second thought and even feel ignored. Not surprisingly, this caused me to really dislike football. Imagine my reaction when many years later I married a Dallas Cowboys' football fanatic. I loved Montell, but instantaneously found myself having old, familiar feelings of being a second thought and feeling ignored each and every year when football season came around. I endured it for several years because it was "his thing," yet those childhood feelings would always come back, just like the football season.

We finally addressed his behavior several years into this pattern and both determined that if he were to place his hobby in its proper place and not allow it to take priority over God, myself, our kids, our church, our family and friends and his job, I may even be able to enjoy the sport again. He gave it a try. He found times to set his team up that didn't interfere with family time. Even when a game was on and he was with me, *he was with me.* A win or loss didn't affect his attitude and he would even begin asking me my thoughts on which players he should put in the game from week to week. Even though that was not my passion or hobby, *he invited me into something he would do, making it something we could do.* Just knowing I am invited into his world assures me that it is still our world. To my surprise, I actually love football now! Our youngest son Skyler is playing in the state league and you had better believe I am the loudest, most fanatical mom in the stands yelling, "That's my baby!!!"

[MJ] Pastor Dennis Rouse often says, "We are all born selfish." As babies, we have a constant need to be fed, burped, changed, and cuddled. For some reason, many of us carry those exact same needs right into manhood! We are brought up to be providers and have our own things. Many men don't even understand why leaving the toilet seat down is such a big issue, as we selfishly and territorially want to have our way. It's easy to get lost in the world of video games, sports and outdoor activities. However, getting lost in that world at the expense of neglecting or losing what we have in the real world is a cost no man should desire to pay.

It's okay to have some "me time" in life. You need it and your wife will need it as well. Although we may not understand why they would ever want to be away from us, those little escapes and breathers are healthy when in the proper position. Creating more of these things you both can do together is a definite win in this area as well. It doesn't have to be expensive or fancy, either. Kristin and I like to have what we call "movie marathon" days. We will find discounted tickets, go to the dollar theater, and see at least 4 movies back-to-back in one day! We watch an action flick for me, chick flick for her (and secretly me), and two other box office or recommended films we agree we want to see. These are normally great days, as we are able to spend selfish time together. Marriages grow when you commit to spending selfish time together.

[MJ & KJ] This may be a drastic change for the newly married folks or perhaps even those who have been married for a while and have fallen into some unhealthy patterns. Although challenging, you really can reevaluate your priorities and watch your life line up with God's will for your life.

Keep in mind that this change is not a one-time deal. Because it is so easy to fall back into old patterns, this shift in priorities will need to be in your mind 24/7. Whenever things start getting a little haywire in our home, we begin evaluating if our priorities are in alignment. Nine times out of ten, the problem or disruption can be sourced back to a priority being out of alignment. Don't sweat it. Simply re-evaluate your list and make the adjustments you need to get back on track. Remember, the blueprint is for you to follow, not rearrange; a roof of a house can't be in the basement, can it? If it works, work it. God, spouse, kids, church, family and friends, career and personal interests.

We'd love for you to share. There is a blog to give your testimony and encourage others at www.montellandkristin.com, where we invite you to be a part of sharing your personal transformation stories for what happens when the blueprint is shifted after you and your spouse put first things first. We are witnesses that God's plan works. Will you share?

CHAPTER 4

Covenant vs. Contract

[MJ & KJ] As we continue to explore the architectural design of the blueprint, we want to really take the time to focus on the God principle, the cornerstone on which all of life is built. This is the most important rock that everything else hinges on and a constant reminder that will always get us back on track when we seem to lose our way while navigating the sometimes uncertain and uncharted waters of marriage. Here it is:

"Marriage is a covenant relationship between 3 people: you, your spouse and God."

We are aware that for many, this is a completely new concept. This is a stark contrast from what the world tells us. We are familiar with the idea of, "This is between you and me." The reality is that when we enter into the covenant of marriage, the Holy Spirit is the power that joins us together and confirms the union. He seals the deal. Yet often in the marriages of both Christian and non-Christian couples, we function as though the third party (God) is not even in the room. We make decisions based on the feelings of two emotionally charged people (sometimes one) without consulting or asking approval from the only solid and eternal thing knitting us together.

Let's explore this idea of covenant vs. contract.

The Merriam-Webster Dictionary provides multiple definitions for marriage and cites how today's culture redefines marriage as "a binding agreement between a man and a woman, in an arrangement, or a consensual or contractual relationship recognized by law."[4]

In most parts of the world, marriage is considered a legal union with members of the opposite or even the same sex. If by definition marriage is simply a contract between two people, consider this:

-Anything bound can be **unbound**

-Agreements can end in **disagreement**

-Arrangements can be **re-arranged**

-Something consensual can be **nonconsensual**

-Laws can change, making legal unions **illegal**

-Contracts can be **negotiated, amended and broken**

Marriage is not a contract. It is a covenant and it is everlasting. Everything we have discussed so far rests on this covenant mentality. Men look at marriage as a contract; God sees marriage as a covenant. Man did not create marriage, God did.

In a resource provided by Victory World Church called *Married Forever*, Anthony and Phyllis Breech document in the Marriage Covenant section several other differences between contract and covenant.

A contract is often limited liability, meaning until I'm not happy; a covenant requires unlimited responsibility, meaning, no matter what. Contracts are conditional in nature, meaning 50/50 whereas a covenant is unconditional in nature, meaning 100/100. A contract is convenience based; yet a covenant is commitment based. They also list the law of priority (First things first from the previous chapter) as the most important value in upholding the marriage covenant.

[KJ] I'll say it again because it's worth saying again: A Godly marriage is a covenant, not a contract. We are to take the same stance regarding our marriage as God takes when He makes a covenant with his people. Covenants last forever.

Think of the covenant God made with Abraham. It transcends generations, it is irreversible, and it stands to this day. When God's chosen people lost their way, forsaking Him by worshiping idol gods, He wanted to erase them from the face of the planet and start over, but He couldn't. He had made a covenant with them and God does not break a covenant. Contracts, promises, dreams, ideas, agreements, arrangements and civil unions all may be breached and broken. A covenant is eternal. How can a marriage be between 3 people? God math.

Since God math is a subject you probably never studied in school, let us give you a brief lesson. If you have read any of the stories in the Bible, I am certain you would note that man's math and God's math are not the same. For example, remember when Jesus takes the five loaves and two fish and multiplies them and they somehow become enough to feed 5,000? That is a different kind of math. Recall when Jesus fed the crowd of 4,000 that had been following him for three days by taking seven loaves and a few fish and still had seven baskets left over? That same kind of math is what God uses when He enters into a marriage covenant with us. I am a student of math. I absolutely love numbers, so these kinds of nonsensical equations really challenge my way of thinking. However, after all the things I have experienced in my life, I have come to accept God math is just different than man's math. Now, I am so glad it is.

God math is not like what we are taught growing up in kindergarten. For example, in school we were taught that 1+1=2. However, in God math, 1+1=1. *"For this reason a man will leave his father and mother and be united to his wife, and the two will become one flesh.' So they are no longer two, but one flesh. Therefore what God has joined together, let no one separate,"* (Mark 10:7-9, NIV).

Another example is 1+1+1=1. *Ecclesiastes 4:12 (NLT)* says that *a triple-braided cord is not easily broken.* A covenant marriage that is submitted to the Lord reflects this equation. Three separate strands, each spouse and the Lord, are woven together as one cord to be used for His purpose. It is in this three-fold cord that we, through marriage, are in our closest resemblance of our Father. We mirror the imagery of the Holy Trinity of the Father, the Son and the Holy Spirit. This is what a covenant looks like and why we are instructed not to enter into marriage lightly.

On the other hand, contracts are often entered into with the expectation that it may possibly or eventually result or end in divorce. I worked in the music business for nearly 20 years so I have seen my share of contracts, most of which are entered into based on what is best and convenient for each individual. It's usually entered into with a specific amount of time in mind and sets the terms for which someone may exit the contract. Another condition of a contract is that it is based on the performance of the other party in the agreement. In the event the performance or expectation is not lived up to, the other has the right to terminate the contract.

Do these terms of agreement resemble any marriages you know?

[MJ] Know with whom you are entering into a covenant. The covenant is a commitment not only to your spouse, but also with the Lord. It is a relationship between the three of you. It is where both parties give all of themselves sacrificially without our own interest in mind, always preferring our spouse's interest over our own, and the third party, the Holy Spirit, bears witness for us. It is not self-seeking or selfish but rather a commitment to be sub-mitted, humble, meek and kind to one another. We do this not because we always feel like it, but because we made a commitment in the presence of the Lord. No time frame or statute of limitation can be placed on it because it is a forever commitment. It is not based on the *if-then* principle (if she does this, then I will do that), but rather on my commitment regardless of receiving the desired result from my spouse.

Many people enter into marriage with an exit strategy opposed to an eternal strategy. Unfortunately, the mindset going into the relationship is often focused on, "If this doesn't work, then this is how I get out." That is not covenant mentality. It is not surprising that so many marriages don't succeed when understanding the covenant, God's promise and cornerstone of the blueprint, is the entire foundation upon which marriage is built.

When God looks at our marriage, He only sees one person. This is why we are called to submit in the relationship. God is the head of the marriage, not the man. As the man submits to God, the woman may safely submit to the man. Our wives are called to walk alongside us, not behind us. However, there can still only be one head. Anything that has more than one head is normally known as a "freak," and we don't mean that in a good way!

1 Peter 3:1 says "Wives, in the same way submit yourselves to your own husbands so that, if any of them do not believe the word, they may be won over without words by the behavior of

their wives, when they see the purity and reverence of your lives."
I am required to lay down my life for Kristin just as Christ died for
the church. Kristin is only required to submit to me; she doesn't
have to die. Ladies, this means you actually get the better end of
the deal! Wives are to be submitted to their husbands, yet we as
husbands must lay down our lives. Wives, the reason God has you
submit to your husband is because as the head, we are ultimately
held accountable for our marriages. This is why it is so important
to know whom we are uniting with. We are not just signing up to
get married, but signing up to follow the Lord so we may lead our
spouse. So, here's the thing. Wives are encouraged to follow their
husbands as they are submitted to follow Christ and trust the God
in them to lead. The direction always comes from the head.

[MJ & KJ] We may have mentioned that our marriage started on
a rocky foundation because there were not a lot of healthy examples around us to show us how to do the marriage thing well. We
had seen many examples of how not to do it (no pun intended)
but as we grew in the word, we had to deliberately seek out God
principles in order to develop core beliefs and truths to solidify
our initial foundation.

After reading this chapter, you may be asking if your marriage
resembles a covenant or contract. You may even question if your
spouse is the one God chose for you or the one *you* chose for you.
Mark 10:9 says, "Therefore what God has joined together, let no
one separate." Our pastor, Dennis Rouse, has a way of saying that

"Without God, I am nothing, I have nothing and I can do nothing." In essence, outside of Jesus, we are no one. We repeat: Outside of God, we are no one. When the scripture says to let no one split apart what He has joined together, it means no one *outside* of the marriage and no one *inside* of the marriage (even you)! We don't mention this to open a conversation regarding divorces and remarriages. This book is mostly for those seeking to enhance their current or future marriage, not to condemn anyone who may have experienced a previous separation. So, even if you are someone who has experienced a prior marriage, take advantage of the opportunity to make your marriage an eternal covenant and not a contract.

When we counsel young couples, we specifically ask them if they believe they heard the Lord confirm to them that this is their mate. If they are not certain, we will suspend further meetings until they get that confirmation. The reason we are waiting for that confirmation is because if the Lord said it, we never have to revisit half of the conversations that will come up in the future. With so many resources available to determine if God has called them to be joined with someone (our church provides Married Life, Pre-Married Life, and everything Jimmy Evans ever wrote), by the time they reach us for counsel that should be the one thing of which they are certain. Did God say this is your husband? Did God say this is your wife? Otherwise, when trial comes, you will find yourself asking unproductive questions like, "Did I marry the right person?" or "I wonder what it would be like if I had married ..."

When you get a confirmation from the Lord and trial comes (not *if*, but *when*) instead of wondering "what if," you are only trying to figure how to resolve the issue and get through it (not over it) so you can get on with your lives, allowing that test to become the beginning of your test-imony. Seeking the Lord in regards to who you are to marry removes the doubt of your decisions and helps you make wiser choices in the midst of challenging situations. Confirmation helps you overcome obstacles in marriages such as doubt, boredom, and incompatibility. Over the years we have counseled many couples who have often identified these things as reasons they have divorced or have contemplated divorce. If you are reading this and contemplating marriage, we implore you to wait until you both hear from God regarding the one He has chosen for you. He wants to give you the desires of your heart. Seek Him first. If you seek the spouse first, you may find yourself backtracking to ask Him to bless the desires of your heart, which may not be His desire for you.

Now, for those of you who may have gotten married but didn't ask God if that was your mate, the good news is God knew you would make the choice you did and He is the redeemer of mankind. This means He can bless something even if it looks like a mess. Your journey to resolution may be a little different, yet His promises are the same. The blueprint is not only a solid, foundational marriage-building tool but also a foolproof restructuring tool. God is king of renovating and rehabbing our marital properties!

According to His word in Isaiah 55:8-9, *our thoughts are not His thoughts and our ways are not His ways.* Therefore, the honoring and acceptance of His covenant over our contract/commitment, regardless of what we think and feel, affords us the opportunity to use the same design to build our marriages starting from where we are right now. God can use *any* decision we have made, good and not so good, for His glory. However, we must allow Him to take over that relationship and be in control of it. He can turn our spouse into the person we need or desire them to be based on our faithfulness. We can't change people; God changes people.

When you entered your marriage, did you have a contract or a covenant in mind? After reading this, do you feel differently? Whether we acknowledge it or not, marriage is *always* a covenant. If we now know that we have entered into a covenant thinking it was simply a contract, some reprogramming and renewing of our minds may be on the agenda. Perhaps you will consider reconstructing your thought process from contract mentality to covenant mentality. Our government is making legislation regarding marriage based on it being a contract, not a covenant. Based on our own childhood experiences and pre-conditioning, we often see contract over covenant. The opinions of our friends, family members and even our parents often value contract over covenant. We have concluded that God's word regarding marriage trumps all the other voices, laws and personal opinions. Covenants are everlasting.

As married couples, let's subscribe to the timeless words of an old song from Al Green and "Let's Stay Together." If that's going too old school for you, our friend and R&B crooner Keith Sweat once cried in a song, "Make It Last Forever." In other words, since marriage is a forever thing, it makes sense to make it the very best forever possible. It all comes down to choice. We have the power to choose and we can choose to win. The time, effort and attitude that we put into our covenant will result in what we will ultimately get out of it. Then, the third party in the marriage (God) adds the extra blessings on top!

So what have you committed to? Are you in a covenant or a contract? Are you seemingly committed to your marriage knowing there are loopholes that exist allowing you to exit? Are you content that forever can be redefined as "forever... until?" Are you and your spouse willing to consider viewing your marriage as something eternal over what is currently existent? Reflect on what you have said you would "do." Pray together that your "I don'ts" won't outweigh your "I do's." Consider internally reviewing and renewing your marriage vows to see an external manifestation of this internal change become activated in your marriage. Both you and your spouse will feel and see the difference.

CHAPTER 5

DLYO- Don't Leave Yourself Options

[MJ & KJ] Kristin and I often raise eyebrows when public speaking as we boldly proclaim that we will be married to each other, together, forever. We state that there is nothing that either of us has done, is doing, or will ever do that will cause us to separate. We then continue to state that we know this to be a non-negotiable truth, along with the fact we will never divorce. How can we say this? It is only through our acceptance of God's word and embracing the covenant mentality that we can venture to make such a bold disclaimer. Without fully digesting the covenant ideal of marriage, there will always exist the possibility of separation or divorce. Many reading this right now may have experienced divorce, be products of divorce or possibly be entertaining the idea of divorce. We submit to you that despite our previous encounters with divorce, God loves and adores us. The termination of a marriage does not stop God's love for us. Whether through seemingly good choices gone bad or bad choices gone worse, Jesus loves us because of who He is and not what we do. There is nothing that we can do that will make Him love us any more and there's nothing we can do that will cause Him to love us any less. Please understand this. God loves us… but He hates divorce. Malachi 2:16 makes it pretty clear, "God hates divorce."

[MJ] When God designed the covenant of marriage, He intended it to be forever. Kristin and I have fasted, prayed, studied and inquired of God for a remedy regarding how it is possible for a married couple to stay together forever. In a world full of temptation, fallible people, lusts, adultery, weakness, suggestive marketing in everything from TV commercials to cartoons, music to movies, social media (currently Facebook, Instagram, Pinterest, Twitter) and a bombardment of endless materials the enemy has presented to entertain us and our flesh, we felt God saying that solving this complex problem requires a simple solution: D.L.Y.O. *Don't leave yourself options.*

We want to share with you right now where we stand on this issue and believe the word of God will confirm this to you: divorce is *not* an option. We know that statement might offend some of you, yet throughout all our personal life experiences, we have yet to find where divorce has been something praiseworthy. Understand what we are suggesting. Even if divorce is an available option, we have the option to remove it as an option! We are able to say we will be together forever because we have taken the option of divorce completely off the table. If in your marriage divorce is currently an option on the table, remove it. We both agreed that when we said, "Till death do us part," we were entering into a covenant, not a contract and not an option. This also meant we weren't allowed to kill each other either (this is also not an option).

Scholars present a compelling argument that the Bible does present acceptable grounds for divorce and honestly, you don't have to be an intellect to read where it says that in the word. However, we believe that if those acceptable grounds for divorce are eliminated from the equation, we will never need to walk that pathway even if the option is available to us. God reconciles. Citing irreconcilable differences as a means to divorce while under His Lordship means that either He is not the God He says He is or His power is not enough to heal our issues. God's power is not enough to heal our human issues? The word allows for a way out, yet also provides an explanation for the loophole. In the book of Matthew, Jesus answers the question of some religious leaders trying to entrap him and clarifies that although Moses instituted the concessions allowing divorce, it was never God's original intention.

"Then why did Moses say in the law that a man could give his wife a written notice of divorce and send her away?" they asked. Jesus replied, "Moses permitted divorce only as a concession to your hard hearts,

but it was not what God had originally intended."
Matthew 19:7-8

Moses permitted divorce. As we researched looking for the origin of divorce to determine where this torrid path began, we found in Deuteronomy chapter 24 the laws regarding reasons permitting divorce. We believe that Moses didn't just invent this idea and pass the law on his own; he was God's messenger and therefore if Moses permitted it, it could only be because God allowed it. Jesus said God allowed it because of the "hardness of their hearts," (Matthew 19:7-8). We ask you to consider a few things. We are permitted to divorce. If you desire to go duck hunting, go fishing or simply drive your own car to the local market, you need a permit. If you don't have a permit, there's no hunting, no fishing, and no driving. Not everyone desires to hunt, fish or drive, so a permit is not always needed. This means that even though a permit is available to them, they have the option *not* to have that option.

When the divorce permit is taken off the table, we have greater opportunity to experience God's faithfulness to heal, restore and transform us. We can become people who know the height, depth and width of the forgiveness He has for us as we show it to our spouses. If we are still considering divorce as an option, there is a chance there still is a hardening of the heart that has not yet been healed. Jesus asks us for that opportunity to heal us and show that in our weakness, He is made strong. When it comes to divorce, it takes your strength to leave but it takes God's strength to stay.

In no way do we believe that someone should stay in an abusive atmosphere or in close proximity to life-threatening situations. We believe the Lord knows whom these passages are for and as they are read He will reveal if this message is specifically designed and personalized for the person reading. This means we have also experienced marriages being restored where physical abuse was once present. We do not recommend or condone remaining in harm's way. God's healing power may occur up close and personal or possibly from a distance in situations where physical abuse was or is present.

[KJ] I come from a background that includes several divorce experiences. Along this literary journey I will share more of my story regarding my parents. Because of this history, I personally understand why although God allowed the exit from marriage; He did so with the disclaimer that staying in the marriage and reconciling (working it out) is the better option. Personally speaking, there is nothing good that comes of divorce. It leaves a path of destruction that is not easily forgotten, erased or recoverable. I am a witness.

When we don't leave ourselves options and take the dreaded d-word off the table, the bumps along the way are a bit smoother. If we know that neither of us is going anywhere, we will certainly disagree a little more fairly and think more carefully about the way we treat, speak and handle each other.

Here's an example. If you know you need your job and yet your boss is rude and disrespectful to you, how would you handle it? Would you get loud and indignant and just walk out? Or would you suck it up and keep it moving, knowing that you need that job to pay your bills? Would you find a way to make it work? You would probably tolerate it for as long as you could, waiting for the first opportunity to quit.

Often times we treat our spouse like we do our job, just enduring each day, waiting for the moment when we can "get out." In the covenant of marriage, there is no such thing as an "out." That's why we must treasure and nurture our marriage so it will last and get better with time.

When my husband and I host "Marriage Masterpeace" seminars, one of the things we teach is how marriages are like rivers of flowing water. In order to maintain a healthy water flow, our marriage should be filled with healthy two-way communication. This is when we listen and not fuss, love and not lash. Our water should be filled with paying attention to the things that are important to our spouse and learning how to nurture them in their love language (we will discuss this more in Chapter 10). The water should be filled with being conscious of their needs and facilitating what is in our ability to do, preferring them over ourselves. When our relationship is filled with these things, it allows a marriage to flow freely and function healthily.

In a Godly marriage, the water is always flowing. There should not be a breakdown in communication. In our experience, we would say we see more marriages end in divorce due to lack of communication than financial pressures and even unfaithfulness. Consider this: if the flow is not a two-way stream, a reservoir forms. This is like a retention pond, a place where the water becomes stale and contaminated due to water flowing in with no place to flow out. Are you a spousal retention pond? Do you receive things from your spouse and not allow it to flow back to supplement the original source? In this blueprint, the Holy Spirit is the source where we replenish and get fresh water to keep the continuous flow between our spouses. Montell and I refer to this place in our marriages as a "spiritual dam."

A dam is a barrier constructed to prevent the flow of water and raise its water level, usually to serve a purpose such as generating electricity to power an entire city. This is a very important structure to maintain in your life in order to not flood the city below you (or deplete your marriage of the things that keep it intact). In order to ensure the safety of the dam, you have to make sure there are no cracks in it. You repair any breaches or cracks in the dam by eliminating things that could undermine the integrity of the structure. What are some of the things that can cause us to have cracks in our spiritual dam?

[MJ & KJ] Here are 10 points that represent potential "cracks in the dam" which we should avoid in our marriages:

1. Separate Bank Accounts

Ugh! We can hear groans all over the world even as these words are being read. The reality is when God entered into a covenant with us He now views us as *one*. Separate bank accounts suggest that there is still the idea of *your* money and *my* money instead of *our* money. We have difficulty with this concept only if we see ourselves as divided or separate from our spouse. We have found this to be extremely challenging, especially from formerly independent, newly married couples who are used to having "their own." Many young women who have done well in business and who contribute more financially to the household than their husbands seem to hold fast to this mindset. Not functioning as one lends to selfish and individualistic thoughts rooted in the idea of a contract, not a covenant. *No separate bank accounts.*

2. Prenuptial Agreements

Ultimately, this is saying that from the beginning, we are expecting this to end.

[MJ] As an R&B artist with a recording contract from Def Jam Records, I had concerns about getting married. In December of 1993, I signed the recording agreement and received a small advance to begin working on the *This Is How We Do It* album. Two months later on February 14th 1994, Kristin and I got engaged and exactly four months and three days later, we were married on June 18th, 1994. Now, I had plenty of legal advisors, label personnel, friends, fraternity and family all concerned that I should have a pre-nup in place and believe me, they shared their opinions plenty of times during those four months prior to saying "I do." However, despite growing fame and wealth and amidst the Hollywood backdrop of sob stories and tabloid tales of what could happen if I didn't protect myself, I chose to trust God and it was never, ever mentioned to her. I chose not to make it an option.

We were building a life together so no matter who had more coming into the marriage, once we were united, *together* we had it all! In other words, if you feel you need a prenuptial agreement a) that's probably the spouse you are choosing for you, not the one God designed for you and b) you're probably going to need it. In the hip hop song "Goldigger," rapper Kanye West encourages men, "If you ain't no punk, holla we want prenup! We want prenup! Yeah!" Well, fortunately *this* punk has been married for 20+ years, has now five God-sent kids and I'm happier than I've ever been. What are we shouting? *No prenup!*

3. My Friends and Your Friends

[MJ & KJ] Life before marriage can provide extreme difficulties in life after marriage when the relationships we fostered prior to saying "I do" do not adequately involve both spouses. We need to make sure that as we move forward in our marriages that we have mutual friends that have similar interests, goals and a spiritual compatibility. Often we see young couples and even remarried couples that have maintained pre-marital close relationships with friends that are still single or divorced. We are advocates for maintaining loyal friendships, but not at the cost of our marriage.

[MJ] I have a friend who was one of the closest men to me in my life. There was a long period of time when we had to separate as the dynamic of our friendship had to change. We reconnected our families over the last few years, yet our friendship is completely different from our childhood days. All the way up through high school, beyond college and fraternity life, this friend was loyal, almost to a fault. If I had ever committed a crime (I haven't, by the way), he's the type of guy who would help me hide the body. I also knew that if I ever was unfaithful in a relationship, he was the kind of friend who would never reveal my secrets. He would take it to the grave with him rather than betray me as a friend. We all want or probably have a friend like that, right? Well, God revealed to me that in order for me to be faithful to my wife, I needed to have someone to hold me accountable.

Both my wife and I had to sever many relationships that were not nurturing our marriage. Quite honestly, Kristin and I both spent many years feeling like we could not connect with other married couples, mainly because in the music business world we functioned in, there were no outwardly, visible, happily-married Godly couples for us to learn with and from. Even though we had each other, we endured a season of loneliness in order to remove who *we* wanted and allow them to be replaced with who *He* wanted in our lives. In God's faithfulness, He then provided (in His timing) friends that know and support the fact that Kristin and I are best friends first. From that foundation, we are then able to share relationship with others God sends into our lives.

I do not have friends that my wife does not know about, nor do I have relationships of which she is unaware. My friends are her friends and vice versa. Separately, we both have accountability where we seek wise counsel and mentorship, yet we both know who each other's accountability partners are. If we feel we must go outside of our marriage to have friendships to satisfy unfulfilled or unmet desires within our marriages, it can result in division (die-vision) and ultimately may result in a crack in the dam. That slow leak could lead to divorce when relationships outside of marriage seem more satisfying than within. Don't entertain the idea of isolated or exclusive friendships. *Only 'our' friends.*

4. Secrets or Unrepented Sin

Luke 12:3 helps us understand that anything done in darkness will eventually come into the light. Unrepented sin and secrets only lead to guilt, shame and condemnation, which lead to a road of more sin and covering it up. Man condemns us; the Holy Spirit convicts us. Our friend Ricardo Sanchez says, "The enemy knows our name but calls us by our sin; God knows our sin but calls us by our name." Both Kristin and I have experienced the weight of living with unchecked sin in our lives and it is literally like walking around with a cinder block chained to your feet. Furthermore, if these behaviors continue over an extended period of time, the lies compound and keeping up with the façade becomes more complex. Jesus provides a freedom from all of our pasts that no other deity provides. The choice is ours to remain a slave to sin or to be liberated from bondage. Secrets and un-repented sin can cost us everything, yet the price for our freedom cost Him everything. In this trade, or great exchange, we get the better end of the deal. *No keeping secrets and hidden sin.*

5. Unresolved Conflict

The word says to not let the sun go down on your wrath.

> Ephesians 4:26-27 (NLT) *And "don't sin by letting anger control you. Don't let the sun go down while you are still angry, for anger gives a foothold to the devil."*

When unresolved conflict takes root within us and begins to grow, it becomes hatred and bitterness and results in a hardened heart. Like unkempt weeds, this ultimately begins choking the life out of our spirit. We are encouraged to choose to operate in love, as it covers a multitude of sins according to the word. Kristin and I made a decision to never go to bed angry, a decision that is embedded deep within us as one of the greatest ways we strengthen our covenant together. From experience, when we go to bed angry, we tend to wake up even more upset and frustrated than the night before, not to mention the fact that tomorrow is not promised to anyone and if for some reason our spouse or we ourselves were called from this life during the night, the effect it would have on the remaining spouse could be devastating. Carrying around unresolved conflict is heavy, yet carrying regret is even *heavier*. So often the slightest misunderstandings lead to the greatest debacles, as the enemy doesn't need much room to get in. He doesn't even need a foothold; just a pinky toe is room enough for him to sow strife, bitterness, malice, mistrust, and begin the process of eroding the dam structure in efforts to breach the wellspring of living water needed to sustain a happy marriage. *No unresolved conflict.*

6. Emotional Decision-making

[KJ] We all know we shouldn't allow our feelings to dictate our actions, but this is much easier said than done. Many of us may love our jobs, yet we do not always feel like going to work. As we minister together, we will often hear statements like "I love her, but I'm just not *in love* with her." Or, "Sure, I love him... but I'm just not *in love* with him." We cannot allow how we temporarily feel to dictate our course of action moving forward. Too often, we miss the blessing God has provided for us as we walk away from what He is calling us to. Many married couples don't understand this concept, but hopefully this next statement will open blind eyes to a truth that has been placed right before us in plain sight.

God designed us all to fall in <u>and out </u>of love.

Sounds crazy, right? Well, what might seem even crazier would be if God had created us all to fall in love just one time and that be it. The reality is that God had a romance with His very own chosen people, the Israelites. They were a stubborn people who often turned their back on Him, served idol gods, offering incense and worship to them, and yet time and time again, we find God falling in love with them over and over. That same DNA is within us and as we were created in the image and likeness of our Father, we too were designed to fall in and out of love. Why? So we could experience the joy of falling in love over and over again.

[MJ] I love my wife, and as I am writing this, we are approaching our 21st anniversary. Truthfully, although I love my wife, I have not always felt "in love" with her. This is nearly impossible for any human to do. In those moments when I may not feel like I'm in love, God will do something simple, like allow my youngest daughter to smile or poke her bottom lip out at me. In that moment, I am able to see my wife, reborn. I am able to see some of her mannerisms and quirks as a small baby girl and, through my daughter, experience my wife's childhood years before I ever knew her. Then, something astonishing happens. I find myself falling in love with my wife all over again. There are tons of examples of life moments where we are enabled to fall back in love over and over again. If our hearts are submitted to God, He will show us how to refresh and renew things to love about our spouses over and over again. We must do more than just ask; we must ask *and* wait for the answer. *Do not allow feelings to dictate actions.*

7. Nagging or Verbal Badgering

This crack in the dam can be subtle yet devastating and, over time, compromise the integrity of the structure.

[KJ] Have you ever known someone who seemed to be an eternal pessimist or someone who complained about everything? Somehow, these people are able to find the worst thing about a really good situation. The word says that a wise woman builds her home, but a foolish woman tears it down with her own hands (Proverbs 14:1). A nagging spirit is one of the most destructive devices one can operate with your spouse. It is by our words that our house will be built up or torn down. The words that come from our mouth come from our hearts and are the very thing that can defile us. A woman's words can promote a regular man from klutz to king, ultimately securing her position as the queen. The same formula will work in the opposite.

I remember a time when Montell's career had taken a beating, and the season of fame and finance had drastically changed for our entire family. He was dealing with depression, and the weight of his readjusted ability to provide for our home was taking its toll on him physically, mentally and spiritually. I can still remember referring to him as "My king" even when he didn't behave, resemble or show any signs of kingship. I thanked him for what he did to provide for our family, even when he didn't think it was enough and even when I knew it wasn't enough. God placed me beside him to protect him with my words and as Romans 4:17 says to activate the word of God and "call those things which be not as though they were."

I would begin speaking God's truth for his life into existence, believing God would bring it to pass even when neither of us could see it in the natural. In the natural, we saw obstacles and difficulty, but in the supernatural, He saw greatness and victory. Women, our words are like seeds; whatever we plant into our spouse, positive or negative, will grow. One of the scriptures I could never shake is in Proverbs 21:9, *"It's better to stay outside on the roof of your house than to live inside with a nagging wife."*

Men, as I hear a faint applause, please be reminded that you also carry life and death in the power of your tongue. Your wife is a reflection of you; a well-kept, well-spoken, honoring, confident and gorgeous wife should be a reflection of you. Belittling, badgering and breaking the spirit of your spouse into unhealthy submission is also a reflection of your care and stewardship. A self-conscious, timid, fragile and frigid wife may be a product of your handiwork. God spoke and created our very existence; we have that same ability. God looked at all He had created and said, "It is good." Husbands and wives, take inventory to see what you are creating in your spouse with your words. Can you say, "It is good?" *No nagging.*

8. Harboring Un-forgiveness

[MJ & KJ] This crack is one that will not only break down our marriages, but will also destroy our family, our body, our career, our dreams and most importantly, our relationship with God. When harboring un-forgiveness, our prayers are hindered, rendering us ineffective for our spouse, our family or for the body of Christ. We will explore this in greater detail later on in the *masterpeace*, but the main idea here is that Jesus made the ultimate sacrifice by forgiving us our sins. We didn't deserve forgiveness, yet Jesus did it so that we might have our sins pardoned and have access to eternal life and one day be reunited with our Father in Heaven. When we choose not to forgive, even when someone has wronged us, we, in essence, are saying that what Jesus did for us on the cross is appreciated, but still not sufficient enough to cover our situation. It's enough to cover my sin, but not enough to cover the sins of others. In our marriage, both of us have experienced unfathomable situations where exercising faith in forgiveness through the power of Christ was the only thing that would keep us together.

Do you have faith that what Jesus did for us on the cross was and is enough? Is the power of Christ enough to heal our spouse from a sickness or an addiction? Was His sacrifice strong enough to reform the unchangeable? If so, you will most likely be tested to walk out what you say you believe. Faith without works is dead and belief without action is useless. Let's not just reduce Jesus' actions on Calvary to some really cool thing He did a long time ago and discount the reason *why* He did it. He did it for us so that through His example and power, we could do it for others. *No harboring un-forgiveness.*

9. Unwise Counsel (The Peanut Gallery)

The word says there is safety in the multitude of wise counsel.

"Where there is no counsel, the people fall; but in the multitude of wise counselors there is safety," (Proverbs 11:14, NKJV). We actually enjoy the New Living Translation as well that says, *"Without wise leadership, a nation falls, there is safety in having many advisers."*

Surrounding ourselves with many people who are willing to listen does not necessarily qualify them as wise counsel. Yes, this discounts many of our family members and Facebook friends. Wise counsel= people who fear God (which is the beginning of wisdom). They are appointed (not friended) to our lives and have already achieved where we are trying to go or have spiritual direction in an area we may be physically walking through together. Wise counsel advises you to seek out those with the solutions, not the symptoms. We often say that our achievements are called "success" and our failures are called "experience." We jokingly say we have *lots* of experience to share with everyone, yet understand that our experience is that we stayed together, and so can you!

Let's talk about posting life's difficulties on social media. Eliciting responses from friends who may agree with you, haters who secretly desire to see you fail and a multitude of others who are just spectators, not counselors, is not seeking wise counsel. Social media is a tabloid or a headline, not a journal. Wise counsel has no hidden agenda or benefit in the outcome. Wise counsel does not seek to control or manipulate, but rather to inform and educate.

The "peanut gallery" was a term coined back in the vaudeville era referring to those who came to spectate an event and occupied the cheapest seats available in the venue. Having paid the least amount to view the event and having so little vested interest in the event, the input that often came from the hecklers adding their $.02 of opinion after watching the event from their cheap-seat view was not welcomed. Perhaps some of us should view our social networks the same way. We give people cheap access to our life events with very little vested interest in the outcome. They offer their $.02 as though it is something of great value while all they are doing is viewing the news feed off of their computer monitor, laptop, tablet, cellular phone, or any other "cheap seat" device. When we expose ourselves in this way, we allow our life's journey to become "public events" instead of "personal experiences." *Seek wise counsel.*

10. Best Friends

When we get married, our husband or wife becomes our new best friend. This transition should actually happen prior to saying

"*I do*." This is important because our best friend is the person with whom we share the most important and valued information about our lives. They document our very existence up close and personal and are God's way of testifying that we were alive during the moments to which the rest of the world has no access.

Many couples enter marriage believing they can still retain their previous individual friendships and relationships. The difficulty with this is that within the covenant of marriage, God no longer sees us as our friends see us or how we often still see ourselves. He only sees *one* person. Even the idea that either spouse can have their own group of separate friends insinuates that they don't see themselves as united. We have experienced the frustrations of many couples that have noticed once they got married their friends began to treat them differently. Those friends will comment that marriage "changed" you and you are not the same as you used to be. News flash! This is simply because you *are* different and you are *not* the same as you used to be. Quite honestly, any prior friendships and relationships that do not respectfully begin to see you differently should be considered toxic and a possible candidate for termination or at least deactivated until further notice.

[MJ] As Kristin's best friend, I desire for her to have other close friends as well. It is my desire for her to have relationship and community outside of my presence, yet not outside of my knowledge. She is a great friend and has great friends. As her soul mate, I also know who her closest friends are. I have friends as well, and Kristin knows of every relationship, both male and female, to which I am a party. As we are one, we should have that accessibility and full disclosure to those in proximity of our marriage. The enemy loves to use simple and seemingly harmless opportunities to entangle unsuspecting spouses in situations intended to steal, kill and destroy from just the smallest exposure to any relationship outside of our marriage. This extends beyond members of the opposite sex, but also into those who are closest to us who might be willing to violate the boundary of our spouse being our best friend. This can happen with our mothers and fathers, our siblings, and even our closest relatives, as they will test to see if the validity of our "marriage vows" and our actions will line up.

The danger in not defining our spouse as our closest friend opens the door to rumor, slander, gossip and confiding intimate details with those outside of the covenant relationship. The reality is there is no woman on the planet I should feel safe and comfortable with to share my marital successes and failures with more than my wife, my best friend. No mom, sister, aunt, daughter, grandmother or any other descendent of Eve should stand in this space. There is no man on the planet my wife should feel safe and comfortable with to share our marital successes and failures with more than me, her best friend. No dad, brother, uncle, son, grandfather, priest, pastor or any other descendent of Adam should stand in this space. This is so that when difficulties and disappointments arise (and they will), we are safeguarding against the temptation to speak negatively about our spouse and protecting ourselves from sowing seeds of discord within our marriage. What we sow will grow.

There is not a single detail of my life that I have not shared with my best friend. Imagine that in 20 years of marriage we have personally dealt with bouts with infidelity, addictions, lusts, masturbation, miscarriage and every taboo topic one can think of, yet I am free today as I trusted God and the one He placed beside me to be his representative here on earth, my wife. I need accountability. Every man and woman needs someone to help hold us accountable. I need Kristin in the dark times. My greatest joys and deepest fears can only be shared with the one closest to me. Why settle for the next best thing when we can have the real thing?

We will all experience dark times and, just like high quality film, that's when things are developed -- in the dark. Exposure to light before the picture is fully developed will ruin the photo. Exposing our life outside of the one placed here to develop with us places our final product in jeopardy. If you feel there are relationships and friendships that your spouse wouldn't approve of, I encourage you to explore why you feel that way. Any relationships that both Kristin and I can't agree on will cease to exist with quickness. We value each other and our covenant of marriage more than any external friendship. Even the most loyal and lifelong relationships come under submission of our vows. Consider this before saying, "I do." If you say you do and you really don't, you are potentially chipping away at the infrastructure designed to bring you lifelong happiness. *Know you are marrying your best friend.*

There are limitless other subjects we could bring up regarding this topic, but that will just have to wait for *Marriage Masterpeace II*. These are the top ten most common examples of cracks in the dam that we have witnessed and experienced personally. This list was comprised not only from our lives, but also fielded from Q & A in our seminars where we learned these most often are the cracks used by the enemy to unravel the fabric of marriage. In order to ensure a healthy and happy marriage, it is imperative that we deal with these "cracks" and repair the breach so that our dam can remain intact and the rivers of flowing water remain fruitful, refreshing and strong.

Take a moment after reviewing this chapter and see if any of these 10 potential cracks are compromising the structure of your marriage. If so, what better place to expose these hazards than in the safety of the One who declares that in our weakness, He is made strong? We believe in you and so does God. This is a part of the blueprint. We are now building our marriages upon the principles of God's word, and just like in real construction, an inspector always comes to check the integrity of the structure and its ability to carry the weight of what will additionally be placed upon it. Having these 10 items in check definitely leads to a stronger foundation and secures a permit to continue building.

CHAPTER 6

Environment

en·vi·ron·ment: *the circumstances, objects, or conditions by which one is surrounded. Conditions that influence the life of an individual or community.*

[MJ & KJ] If our environment weren't a critical issue, God wouldn't have told Abram, "Leave your country, your family, and your father's home for a land that I will show you. I will make you a great nation and bless you. I'll make you famous; you'll be a blessing. I'll bless those that bless you; those who curse you I'll curse. All the families of the Earth will be blessed through you," (Genesis 12:1). There was a blessing in the obedience of Abram leaving his familiar surroundings and trusting what God was leading him into. Most miracles don't occur in seasons of comfort and contentment. Abram had to get uncomfortable to become more reliant on God, and so must we.

To expand just a bit more in the area of "your friends and my friends" from the previous chapter, let's explore why it is essential to alter our environment after getting married. We have found that we either become the company we keep or the company we keep becomes us. Are we the influencers or the ones being influenced? Is it strange that God says when we get away from where we are now, away from our family and our parents, *then* He will show us what He has for us? What if Abram had decided he didn't really feel like moving? What if he decided he couldn't live without his family? What if he said, "But God, my mom is my *best friend*? I'm comfortable here. I'm surrounded by friends and family. My life is pretty good just the way it is."

Do you think God would have been like, "Oh yeah, my bad. I forgot you desire to stay comfortable in your familiar surroundings while I bless you"? God's love is unconditional, yet His blessings often come with conditions. Conditional means *when* we do x, y & z, *then* He will administer the promises to us. There's an old hymn that says, "If you take one step, He'll take two." Conditional means we are required to make the first step, and in response to activating our faith, He will then fulfill His part of the agreement. When we do these things, we will receive the blessing and He will make us a great nation that is blessed, He will make us known, and in turn we may become a blessing to those around us. The reality is that everyone can't go where God plans to take us. Many around us are not destined to share in the inheritance God has for you, for even

Christ (who had 12 disciples) sometimes only took Peter, James and John with him. Abraham too had to leave his comfort zone to walk into God's promises. When we are comfortable and content, we often don't think we need a miracle. It's when we are in a place of discomfort or need that we come to expect God to do something remarkable, supernatural or even impossible.

Reading this passage of scripture leads us to believe that if Abraham had desired to remain Abram, and not allow his name and his environment to be changed, he could have never walked into the promise of God. The last sentence is particularly intriguing, as it states, "Because of your obedience *all* the families of the Earth will be blessed," (emphasis all). Hey, guess what? We are a part of *all*! Abraham's obedience way back then is part of *our* inheritance today and the blessing we are entitled to and walking in now! We think it is safe to say that the whole environment thing might be a little bit more important than any of us had originally thought.

[KJ] When we enter into a covenant marriage, it is critical that we change our environment. I can hear the complaints now: "But my family and friends are going to treat me differently if I start changing!" You're right, they certainly will! Do you want to know why they are going to treat you differently? Because you *are* different! We should be different, as we have entered into the next phase of our lives that comes with the promise of favor and blessing only available to those in the covenant of marriage. If attaining God's favor hangs in the balance because you are worried about changing your environment, we implore you to tip the scales and see that God offers more than what we can think or imagine.

Montell and I have witnessed many couples that chose not to adapt their environment to their marriage who are now a part of staggering divorce and separation statistics. Good, loving and kind friends of ours have underestimated the tremendous power that our family, friends, fame, wealth, circumstances and conditions have in determining their destiny. Instead of setting up shop in an atmosphere conducive to winning, many people don't take this godly request seriously and just hope to beat the odds. The results are mostly negative. Tragically, as the census bureau cited in earlier chapters, more than 50% of marriages end in divorce. If you had a 50% chance that when you got in a car that it would start, would you buy that car? We don't want to alarm you, but enlighten you. We encourage the covenant of marriage, still the divorce rate statistics are a reality. Perhaps, like the children of Israel, the covenant is not as important to us as it is to God. God wants to be the greatest influence in our lives, over our friends, family members, children and exes.

[MJ] No one can argue that life for a single person is completely different than for someone who is married. Just go over to one of your single friend's bachelor or bachelorette pad and look around. Our lifestyles are just different. We have different responsibilities, commitments and objectives. When you are single you have a different mindset than you do when you are married. Someone who is single has a different mindset and operates with a different objective in mind. When we were living single lives, we only had to worry about ourselves; once you get married that is no longer an option. When you are married, selfish thoughts are very dangerous and counterproductive. This is not a knock against singles (as they are the perfect candidates to one day be married!). We should have relationships with those who are friends and single, but the boundaries need to change. The reality is that singles can have great success and favor upon their lives, but they will still never attain the level of favor God places on those who find a good thing (a wife) and obtain it (favor) from Him.

Attaining favor is what we are capable of getting on our own; *obtaining* favor is what the Lord gives to us. There is a favor that is unattainable to us outside of Him granting us access to it through marriage. Obtaining this favor requires change. Mark 2:22 reminds us not to pour new wine into an old wineskin. It's extremely challenging to follow this principle when we become a new marriage. Keeping our new marriage in our old lifestyle really is like pouring expensive champagne into an unclean glass. When two become one in the covenant of marriage, any previous relationship that still seeks to identify us as the same individual we once were should become an immediate candidate for early life dismissal. We can't go to the same places, we can't do the same things and our priorities are different. We encourage you by saying to you what we say to our children: Make better choices. This is not saying we are children, yet at times we can be childlike, stubborn and selfish. Believing we cannot change is childish behavior. It's time for married couples that love God to grow up.

"When I was a child, I spoke as a child, I understood as a child, I thought as a child; But when I became a man, I put away childish things," (1 Corinthians 13:11, NKJV). Men and women of God, put away childish things!

Stop confessing what you can't do and start professing what you can! Perhaps it's time for some new "couple" friends that God directs into your life. It is a much healthier environment for you. We are not saying we can't be friends with single friends; we are saying that we as *individuals* should not foster personal relationships outside of the marriage. The dynamics of these relationships to our marriage must change, and we have to be strategic about how we handle it. This could mean that for a season there should be some distance or complete severing of old relationships and even family ties to ensure healthy new patterns that are conducive for our new lifestyle. This is accomplished when we desire what He wants for us more than what we want for ourselves.

[MJ & KJ] Dealing with unhealthy friendships is difficult, yet it may even become more difficult when husbands and wives have unhealthy ties to family members. Some men are extremely close to their mothers. Think of the NFL football games when the camera crew shoots cameo footage of the players on the sidelines after a great play. Most often you will see the player wave into the camera and say "Hi, Mom!" You can probably count on one finger the number of times you have seen a male athlete acknowledge his father. When difficulties arise in the marriage, a husband may seek to get female advice from his mother. The problem with that is our mothers are our mothers, not our wives.

Our best, closest, well intentioned, and well-wishing family members all have one thing in common: none of them are our spouse. Wives, even if our husbands are dead wrong, a mother will support her son. Husbands, even when our wives are clearly in violation of something, her parents will most likely support her. That's what parents are supposed to do. God eliminated the issue of family members having to choose sides in marital issues by saying, *"Therefore a man shall leave his father and mother and be joined to his wife, and they shall become one flesh," (Matthew 19:5).*

This scripture happens just after God creates a helper comparable to Adam. God searched the environment and brought animals to Adam to see what He would call them. He named them, yet Adam still found none of them fitting to suit him. God then causes Adam to fall into a deep, coma-like sleep and takes one of his ribs and forms Eve from his very own body. Adam awakens and is apparently pleased as he goes into the "This is bone of my bone and flesh of my flesh" speech. Or in other words, "Oooooh weeeeee! Girl, you are fine!"

This may be humorous, but it is important for one reason. Adam and Eve at this time were the only two people on the face of the planet. There were no fathers and mothers in existence. Why would the very next verse following Eve's creation and Adam's acceptance of her state that a man should change his family environment by leaving his father and mother and join with his wife when there was no family environment? We repeat: there were no fathers and mothers in existence yet. Jokingly, we believe God knew that before parents even existed they would eventually butt into their kids' business, so He was just simply being proactive. Truly, God seemed to value the relationship between Himself, the husband and the wife and was setting a foundation, or blueprint (even as early as in the 2nd chapter of the 1st book of the Bible), for us to begin marital construction.

While writing this book we read an alarming statistic that we thought we would share, just in case we ever think our environment isn't that big of a deal. In a 2010 article titled "Is Divorce Contagious?" www.abcnews.go.com stated that researchers had conducted a study about divorce and its adverse effects on social groups. Their finding was that, "Being friends with someone who gets divorced makes someone 147 percent more likely to get divorced themselves."[5]

Friends naturally share struggles they are going through, so it does make sense. If we are the least bit unhappy with any piece of our marriage, the enemy will use this as an open door and come in like a flood, taking full advantage of our new thoughts introduced to us by a friend, family member or recent divorcee "kind" enough to share their harrowing experience.

Another reason why God requires us to separate from our families is so that we can start to create patterns of making our spouse most important and the first person in whom we confide. Having "Mama" as the first person we confide in can set us up for marital strife and even failure. This will create tension and insecurity, eventually creating a rift between spouses. If Mama is telling us one thing and our spouse is saying something else, whom do we listen to? Most people have been individuals longer than they have been married; therefore, their default reaction or response to conflict is to sway towards the relationship they have been in the longest. Lord knows this is a difficult decision to make, so He provides a remedy early on; separate from those who are not your spouse and save your sanity. Attempting to follow mom and wife at the same time may cause a man to make split decisions and possibly even develop a split personality to behave one way before mom and another way before his wife.

A double minded man is unstable in all his ways. (James 1:8)

Changing our environment is essential to cultivating good, fertile soil to plant complementary relationships and harvest a healthy marital atmosphere. We need godly people around us to provide wise counsel and accountability and to mentor and challenge us to be greater. We need likeminded couples to walk with us so that we can identify pitfalls and promises to our marriages together. It is important that we start to hang out with friends that have similar interests and aspirations. If these couples don't exist, begin to ask God to bring them into your lives and to bring you into theirs. It is important to find a core group of friends to *do* life with.

For us, we are on a mission this year to have six couples (12 people) minimum with whom we can intentionally spend a wealth of time. Jesus hung with 12, so we figure we can start with that. Please make sure your spouse also likes hanging out with these friends as well. Attempting to maintain a relationship one of you isn't "in" just doesn't work. Just as some people are in our lives for reasons, seasons and lifetimes, this is a *reason* to pursue a different relationship. It stinks when just the girls get along and not the guys and vice-versa. From experience, that can be painful and unrewarding, so in honor of the most valuable commodity we all have -- time -- save yours and theirs and be in season with whom God appoints at the time.

One of our favorite youth pastors, Jeanne Mayo, says, "Show me your friends and I will show you your future." That being the case, what does our future hold? Are we becoming the company that we keep or are they becoming us? What company are we keeping? Is it fertile soil for our marriage or are we trying to cultivate something healthy in a toxic environment?

Reflect on the environment surrounding you. See if it is producing fruit in your marriage. If not, this is a good place to uproot and begin replanting and landscaping around the foundation of our blueprint. We are building something great in our marriages for Jesus and we want it to look good both inside and out.

CHAPTER 7

He Said, She Said

[MJ & KJ] Communication is one of the most critical elements in a marriage. How well we administer this skill greatly impacts how smooth or bumpy our marital ride will be. Clear communication is absolutely vital to how effective our daily journey is walked out. It is no secret that men and women communicate in completely different ways. The "he said, she said" idea simply suggests that we can never fully see the whole picture clearly in our marriages without having both male and female input. Often, men communicate by solving problems and compartmentalizing. Typically, they are task-oriented and focused on the big picture. Multitasking can be extremely challenging, perhaps even foreign. In contrast, women often communicate through emotion and usually have several things happening all at one time. Generally speaking, many women have the capability to multitask and transition from topic to topic in a moment's notice. While women prefer verbal communication, men may say very little and feel they are telling the whole story nonverbally. Although these general characteristics may overlap in some areas, we agree that most times men and women can witness the exact same event and still come to very different conclusions.

When we get married, there is no switch or easy button to push that automatically allows us to see things from our spouse's perspective. This means that communication is a skill we must all learn and cultivate in order to become an effective communicator with our spouse.

[KJ] Montell and I did not always communicate well. Actually, the beginning of our relationship was quite painful. It is through much learning, pain and perseverance that we have become skilled communicators, and truthfully, even 20 years later, we are still learning new ways to improve our communication every day. If we look at the overall blueprint and re-examine the layout, communication could be considered the kitchen area of the design. It's from positive, 2-way communication that we are fed and nourished in our marriages. Marriages that don't exercise this ability well can easily begin to suffer malnutrition. We submit that there are three essential elements to effectively communicating in our marriages: hearing, speaking, and doing. James 1:19 says, "Be swift to hear, slow to speak, slow to wrath."

Hearing. The word suggests we are to be quick to not only listen, but also to actually *hear* what is being spoken and shared with us. Many husbands and wives are listening to what is being said, yet they are not *hearing* the message being communicated. A fundamental truth is that men and women do not hear the same way. Through our research and experience, we have found that men are mostly fixers and women tend to be listeners. The difficulty occurs as we are inclined to initiate communication in the same way we desire it to be communicated to us.

For example, when I had a frustrating day at work, I would come home and begin to tell Montell what infuriated me or made me unhappy on my job. His first inclination is to listen, yet he was listening with the intent of giving me a solution at the end. He was looking to fix my issue. We would later understand he felt like he had failed at communicating with me if at the end of my sharing he hadn't come to my rescue, cracked the code or provided the perfect solution for me. As he offered suggestions and remedies, I would find myself becoming even more frustrated with him than my original work situation because I felt he wasn't hearing me. In reality, when I came to him, I was really looking for someone to just listen to what I was saying, not fix anything. In actuality, him allowing me to audibly talk it out and arrive to my own resolve, conclusions and plan of action was actually helping fix the issue.

It took years for us to come to this realization and finally overcome this obstacle. Perhaps the men reading this are experiencing a similar issue where you feel you are listening and your efforts to assist your spouse only seem to raise her blood pressure and yours at her rejection of your genius solutions. Perhaps my ladies out there are just looking to be listened to, not fixed, and can't seem to share information with your spouse for fear he may storm to your place of business and punch your boss in the face, failing to realize you were just verbally expressing your emotions.

Here is something we can all try, as this worked for Montell and me. I would provide a disclaimer at the beginning of our conversation so he wouldn't have to try and figure out where the direction of our conversation was going. It was as simple as saying something like, "Honey, I am not looking for an answer, but I need to talk this out." By doing this, we are assisting our spouse to be a better communicator and setting up a win-win scenario where we may express ourselves freely and have him feel like he is helping, because he is! Setting up clear boundaries and clear expectations will help set the tone for dialogue where both of you will be communicating and both of you will feel respected and heard.

On the flip side, there are times when we are seeking direct involvement or intervention from our spouse. In these instances, the same introductory disclaimer is needed and will be appreciated. "Babe, I need you to help me in this situation with the kids…" should sound different than, "You'll never guess what happened to me today!" Ladies, taking this simple measure of assisting our husbands by introducing the purpose of the conversation helps transform us from "miscommunication" to *mrs.communication*. (Did you see what I did there?). Husbands, if your wife doesn't clearly communicate her intention prior to conversation, initiating clarity is important. She will appreciate you pausing to ask if she is seeking answers and action or just your sounding board skills. Once this is identified, being attentive, interested and responsive without being suggestive is an art that when executed properly, can lead to masterful communication. As my husband would say, "Are you picking up what I'm putting down?"

[MJ] Let's examine *speaking*. The word suggests we should be slow to speak and/or respond. Although there is no absolute or definitive measure of verbal communication versus non-verbal, in an article provided by the Center for Non-verbal Studies regarding non-verbal communication, one psychologist named Albert Mehrabian submits in his 1971 study that 7% of communication is words and 93% of communication is non-verbal.[6] This suggests that most communication is actually occurring through what is not being spoken. I studied communication at Pepperdine University and learned from Stephen Covey's "The 7 Habits of Highly Effective People" that everything from body language, posture, facial expressions, tone, timing and non-verbal cues can determine how well we communicate beyond our words, and this definitely applies to our spouse.

We currently live in a social media society and much interaction is done via telephone, computer and text messaging, even within marriages. It is extremely important to maintain and cultivate a face-to-face and personal communication dynamic with our spouse. The way that something is presented in conversation is as critical as how it is received; the exact same words (depending on the inflection, tone and posture of the question or request) will garner a different response based on how he/she perceives they are being asked. Simply stated, be intentional and make sure your words and your actions match. Keep in mind, there should always be two sides in communicating a message, sending and receiving. Once we learn how our spouse communicates, we can make adjustments to bring more clarity and be more effective during this interaction.

Here's a glimpse into a typical Jordan conversation involving *miscommunication:*

[KJ]: "Hey honey, what are you doing on Monday evening?"

[MJ]: "I was gonna watch the game and have a few friends over from my fantasy football league."

My wife is now visibly upset. She asked a question and I gave her a simple answer. What is the issue and why am I now in the doghouse over simply responding to her question? Men reading this are baffled and probably asking the exact same question while most every woman understands exactly where I was in error.

I listened to her question, yet I didn't hear what she was saying.

While my answer was honest, accurate and prompt, it was wrong. I was not slow to speak. What I didn't hear in her question was monumental. Remember, often men think big picture while women think in details. I responded without processing the details, the unspoken messages and purpose layered within her inquiry. Here is the actual translation of Kristin's original question:

[KJ] "Hey honey, what are you doing on Monday evening?"

Translation:

[KJ] "Hey honey, I've been missing you lately. You've been so consumed with work and other activities, and I've been so busy with our home, our children and work responsibilities that it feels like life is getting in the way of us doing life together. I have felt neglected and I'm not certain you see me as a priority right now. I am certain you probably already have made plans, but I want to know if I am valuable enough to be considered in the midst of those scheduled things that are important to you. Your response to the question I am about to ask will show me if you are attentive to my state of being or completely unaware of my feelings. At the risk of rejection, knowing that you already have plans for Monday and hoping I am valued above those plans, I place my heart into a seemingly harmless question. So, here goes. Honey, what are you doing Monday evening?"

[MJ] Wow. Husbands are reading in disbelief right now as wives are praising God that someone finally gets it. Well, it's taken us 20+ years to gather this information and hopefully shift the marital learning curve in favor of bettering communication between husbands and wives. I listened to what she said and in being slow to speak, I was able to process what I really needed to hear from her. This enabled me to cancel my plans with the boys, set my fantasy football roster ahead of time and create a healthy Monday night environment with my wife. After seeing my willingness to sacrifice my interests on her behalf, I have found she now values the value I place on these times and she will often either watch the games with me or happily embrace me spending time with my sons or friends.

[MJ & KJ] From the examples above, here are some suggestions for rules of engagement toward *doing* more effective communication:

1. *Listen* to your spouse and take the time and effort to *hear* what he/she is saying.

2. Communicate truthfully and authentically (avoid the words "never" and "always").

"You *always* put your friends before me."

"You *never* let me do what I want to do."

Those generalities may lead to heated dialog. Replace those general words by expressing how you feel, not what you think your spouse intentionally or unintentionally did.

"I feel there are times your friends are placed before me."

"I feel there are times when my desires to do things are not considered." Transitioning from shifting blame to expressing how you feel assists you to communicate more truthfully and authentically.

3. Timing matters. Be slow to answer after hearing what is actually being communicated. Also, check the spiritual and emotional climate prior to presenting a topic for discussion. The right topic presented at the right time will most often get the right or desired answer.

4. Men and women communicate and hear differently. Communicate the message how you desire it to be received over how you desire to deliver it.

5. Remain engaged in what your spouse is saying- *no* multi-tasking, texting, yawning, looking at your watch or drifting off. Stay engaged while your spouse is speaking as your nonverbal cues can speak more than your actual words.

6. Spouses don't read minds. It is important to communicate your intentions and present disclaimers to clear up any ambiguities in the purpose of your communication.

7. Allow your spouse to speak freely. Don't interrupt. It hinders them from wanting to communicate in the future.

8. *Respect* is always at the foundation of good communication. You are speaking to your best friend and biggest advocate. Watch your tone, and don't speak harshly or down to each other.

9. In the event you do speak harshly, repent immediately and never let it linger.

10. If you are angry and don't know how to communicate, take a break (pray) and then continue so you can communicate our thoughts, disagreements and disappointments in love. When we ask God to give us the words and actually wait for Him to do so, it will be in *love*. Husbands and wives... *Please!* Let's give our spouses the room to communicate in their language, not ours.

Let's take a look at wrath, or anger. This is huge, because some spouses need time to cool off while others feel the need to come to resolution immediately.

In one couple we worked with, the wife would get upset and need time to process so that she didn't say harsh things in the heat of battle that she would later regret. How she was raised and the cultural impartation of how to resolve issues formed her personal blueprint for conflict resolution. The husband, having a different cultural upbringing and conflict resolution experience, felt the need to stay in the heated moment seeking immediate resolution, which would escalate the disagreements into full blown arguments... and sometimes separate sleeping arrangements. In our counseling with them, we asked her if knowing he desired immediate resolution, would she consider not taking extended hours and days before coming back into a discussion. We asked if he would consider giving her the time to process her thoughts, enabling her to bring clearer ideas and word choices into their tough discussions. Together, they were able to find a healthy middle ground to fight fair. When conflict arises, they still must remind each other that she needs time to process while he is seeking resolution. While he is seeking resolution, he must still provide space for her to process.

This is now a part of their communication and a part of being swift to hear, slow to speak and slow to wrath. This adds to the durability of marriages designed to last a lifetime. This husband and wife are now a happily married couple. Even their passionate and spicy heated discussions, when communicated effectively, translate to passionate and spicy intimacy, eliminating the need for separate sleeping arrangements.

[KJ] My husband is what I will refer to as an "over communicator." This means that communication of each detail is very important to him. Even in sharing a simple day's experiences, he must craft each moment as though he were writing a song to make sure every aspect of what he is communicating is heard. It is critical that I listen to the details and hear him out completely or he feels like I am listening, but not hearing him. He tells me all the time we cannot just work to get over our problems, but we have to work to get *through* them. If we don't work through our difficulties, they will remain and only come back up when the next issue arises. When we "get over our problems," they only grow like things swept under a rug. We must pick up the carpet, sweep underneath and then re-lay the carpet in order for the footing to be solid, safe and resolved.

I am not saying this is easy. Hear me when I say that I am the opposite of my husband. My mind thinks in detail, but I do not communicate like that. I communicate in "big picture" terms, yet at times I have the expectation that he know the details that are at this point, only in my head. This is why we constantly have to work on communicating intentionally with the other person in mind. Montell has resolved to the fact that he will need to ask me details and prod for a little more information to understand the whole picture and I have resolved to listening and hearing him in detail and remain focused on the message he is telling me. Each time we communicate, we have to be intentional on how we are transmitting and receiving information to remain on one accord. In the beginning it may feel like work, but over time, it gets easier. He knows I am not only listening, but also hearing him. Even when I am extremely direct and to the point, he will ask me to elaborate so he doesn't miss anything.

[MJ] Here is another example of how Kristin and I seek to complement each other in communicating. I am a champion of "softening" difficult messages, whereas sometimes my wife is not. Even something as simple as sending emails to communicate a message to team members requires us to work together to make sure how we send and receive messages is communicated well. In a world filled with "he said, she said," miscues and miscommunication, we strive to translate better. Here is an example of an email message Kristin would send out:

Hey everyone. Meeting at the arena today at 3pm. Dress warm. Be on time. –KJ

She would then send this message to me before it is sent out and ask me to revise the message. It becomes this:

Good day everyone! We trust all is well and we are all excited about today's ministry activity. We are all meeting at the previously designated location at the arena promptly today at 3pm. We ask that we all be conscious of time and honor those we are serving by being early. Also please be mindful of the weather, as we will be uniformly attired in warm dress clothes. We love and appreciate serving with you all and are looking forward to an amazing day! -Kristin.

In this instance, Kristin is more of the "big picture" communicator and I am more of the "detailed" communicator. Kristin focused on delivering a message that was clear and concise. Noticeably, the art of brevity is not my portion, yet personalization is. No matter which role we serve in our marital communication (big picture or detailer), clarity is key. In this instance, she was big picture and I was the detailer. Sometimes it's the other way around. The point is that delivering a clear message that isn't tailored to be received well is almost as effective as never sending it.

[KJ] I want to share a little story so we can understand the value and impact of our words.

There was a young man who went around town speaking about his best friend unkindly. One day someone exclaimed, "If that's your best friend, I would hate to see how you would speak about someone you don't like." Reflecting on the words of a stranger, he proceeded to call his best friend and asked him for forgiveness. The best friend, realizing that this man had no idea the magnitude of what he had done, told him that he would be forgiven. However, he added, "I need you to do two things for me. First, go home, take a feather pillow, cut it up, and scatter the feathers to the wind." After he had done so, he should call him back.

Though puzzled by this strange request, the man was happy to be let off with such an easy solution. He quickly went home and cut up the pillow, scattered the feathers, and called the best friend back as requested.

"Am I now forgiven?" he asked.

"Yes, of course you are forgiven, but remember, I have one more request. Go now and gather up all the feathers."

"But that's impossible! The wind has already scattered them," the man said.

"Precisely," the best friend answered. "And though you may truly wish to correct what you have done, to repair the damage done by your words is as impossible as it is to recover the feathers. Your words are out there now, unable to be retracted, even as we speak."

Perhaps we hear this story and wonder if these two are actually even best friends. Is a friendship really a friendship if one person continually speaks disrespectfully about the other? If so, then what about us?

How interesting that the communication or the words we speak to our spouse and "best friend" are often not kind or edifying. We have to be careful and cautious about our words and how we choose to communicate. Once words are spoken, they cannot be retracted. Maybe our parents didn't speak kindly to each other or maybe they didn't speak kindly to us, and because of that, we are not sure how to successfully communicate with our spouse. Be assured it is one of the most important things we *get* to work on in this lifetime. Let's use our words to encourage and lift our spouse up. Words can be spoken in anger and have irreparable effects on the ones we love the most. Oft times it is hard for us to accept the fact that the words we speak can — and often do — significantly damage our "best friend."

[MJ & KJ] We want to impart this imagery or visual that may help us look at how well we are communicating with our spouse. Reflect on going beyond just listening, but actually hearing your spouse. Take time before speaking and seek to understand more than to be understood. This prepares us to do or take the appropriate action to fulfill the purpose of the initiated communication. Let's keep in mind that our spouse is a gift from God. He has entrusted us to care for them, nurture them and water them.

Each time we are communicating with our spouse, we can picture an angel recording every word we say and how we say it. Visualize how that makes the angel and God feel. He will transcribe our message and take each word down, word for word, like a court reporter. Now think about him reading that transcript back to us on the day we sit before The Lord in Heaven. Will we be pleased at the way it sounds when the angel reads it back? Furthermore, will the Lord delight in the way we treated the gift that He gave us? If our response to this thought is "No," "I'm unsure" or "Ouch," then perhaps we want to re-think the way we will treat, speak and communicate with our spouse from this point forward. We understand what he says and what she says won't always translate accurately, but *we* say that we have a translator in the Holy Spirit who makes it possible to be on one accord, reading the same blueprint and building and strengthening the same structure.

How do you and your spouse communicate? Consider being quick to hear, slow to speak and slow to responding or reacting in anger. Speak with your spouse and seek if there are ways you both may communicate better.

CHAPTER 8

Affirmation vs. Confirmation

[MJ & KJ] Undoubtedly, this is one of those chapters that will challenge us. However, when it is all said and done, we pray the impartation God desires to reveal to us is received. When The Lord downloaded these nuggets to us, we didn't understand the magnitude of their importance or how the relevance of comprehending affirmation and confirmation could be destiny altering. It is our hope that we can present this truth with the same clarity that it was revealed to us. Affirmation and confirmation are two elements of a marriage that, when properly administered, can begin to design the higher floors in the blueprint. Let's first discuss both of these in context of the most influential historical figure who ever walked the face of the earth: Jesus. Then, we will personalize the idea of affirmation and confirmation by bringing it back to why they are important in our marriages.

[MJ] A few years ago, I was honored to share a Father's Day message called "Who's Your Daddy?" that dealt majorly with the identity that is given to sons and daughters when confirmed by a father. Affirmation and confirmation are key principles in that message and have remained constant in our marital teaching and studies. To *affirm* something is to declare that it is indeed the truth. *Confirmation* declares the accuracy of what was affirmed or in other words, it confirms the truth, stamps it and approves it. Confirmation validates affirmation. We submit to you that confirmation is authenticated only when administered by *a father* or a respected, father-like male authority figure. This theory will challenge many of our thoughts regarding what confirmation is and who gives it, so allow us to explain what we understand as truth.

Let's begin with an example of a historical account taken from scripture. The story picks up in the New Testament following 400+ years of oppression, bondage and captivity of God's chosen people at the hands of the Babylonians. Israel had gotten to a place where they were out of favor with God and desired to be back in His promises. As they were awaiting the Messiah, there was a lot of talk surrounding who He was and what He would accomplish to set the people free and re-establish His kingdom. The Jewish nation was in expectancy of the coming king who they believed would return Israel to their prominence and right standing in the world as the chosen people of God. Many thought that John the Baptist might possibly be the one, yet he assured the people that although he was the voice crying out from the wilderness for the people to repent, there was another who would come and would take away the sins of the world. John was simply there to help prepare the way. He would speak highly of this Savior that was yet to come and everything he spoke in regard to the Lord was true and accurate. He was affirming the character of the coming Messiah, baptizing and preparing those who would believe in this truth. Then Jesus actually showed up.

John now had the awesome responsibility and honor to baptize the very one he spoke about. John affirmed that Jesus was the Son of God according to what he knew to be truth. All of his statements were true and were affirmations of the truth.

Then John gave this testimony: *"I saw the Spirit come down from heaven as a dove and remain on him. And I myself did not know him, but the one who sent me to baptize with water told me, 'The man on whom you see the Spirit come down and remain is the one who will baptize with the Holy Spirit.' I have seen and I testify that this is God's Chosen One." John 1:32-34 (NIV)*

John gives a testimony, an account and *affirmation* of who Jesus is. But watch this shift in perspective: here is a continued, different account of the same event—

As soon as Jesus was baptized, He went up out of the water. At that moment, Heaven was opened, and he saw the Spirit of God descending like a dove and alighting on Him. And a voice from

Heaven said, *"This is my Son, whom I love; with him I am well pleased,"* *(Matthew 3:16-17, NIV).*

It was not until John baptized Jesus and He came up out of the water when the Father Himself showed up, opened the heavens and declared with the same voice that created heaven and earth to behold that "This is my Son in whom I am well pleased." John testified to who Jesus was and *affirmed* all these things to be true about him: that Jesus would be greater and do marvelous works and take away the sins of the world. John testified and affirmed who Jesus was, *but the Father Himself showed up and confirmed what John was affirming!* True confirmation can only come from the authority in place and in that situation, God was the authority.

That's the difference between affirmation and confirmation: *affirmation presents the facts and confirmation seals the deal.* That authority to confirm is given to the Father. I repeat: The authority to confirm is given to the father.

In another instance accounted in Matthew 16:13-17, Peter (one of the closest and most loyal disciples) and Jesus were engaged in conversation when He asked Peter who men said He was. Peter gave a list of things that people were saying: some say you are John the Baptist, some say Elijah, some say Jeremiah or one of the prophets (Please keep in mind that everything Peter was saying was true and accurate, as he was affirming to Jesus everything the people had been saying).

Jesus then stopped Peter and said, "Who do you say I am?"

Peter answered, "You are the Christ, Son of the living God."

Jesus then confirmed that Peter was right and said, "You could only know that *because my Father told you.*" The affirmations all around town were the things that others said. Peter actually knew the correct answer. Jesus shared with Peter that it was by His Father's confirmation that his revelation about who the Son of God was, was true.

In my final example, I have known many personal friends who were raised in fatherless homes. Against all odds, these single moms raised great sons. I have often argued that these women who are forced to become both mom and dad through whatever circumstances have all but one capability in raising their sons. They can teach a boy to be a kind, gentle, responsible and respectful male. Mothers can affirm all these things into their boys. However, the one thing they cannot teach their boys is to be men. It takes a man to confirm a boy into manhood.

Prisons are filled with little boys who walk around in grown men's bodies, having never received confirmation of manhood from a godly-fatherly male figure. Hospital delivery rooms are filled with little boys in grown men's bodies who never received confirmation into manhood from a father, so they accept manhood from becoming a father. The reality is that becoming a father doesn't make you any more of a man than standing in a garage makes you a car. Fatherhood does not confirm manhood. Sadly, there are also little boys in grown men's bodies standing before the altar and saying, "I do." *They do* agree to all the vows, yet *they don't* under-stand the difficulty a boy has in fulfilling the requirements of a man. I honor every woman who has ever been left to raise a boy on her own. I submit that a crowning achievement in the comple-tion of mothers raising boys to men rests in the blessing of a father, a pastor or a respected male authority enlisted to confirm these sons into manhood.

[KJ] Just like it is true in the previously mentioned scriptural testimonies, the application of affirmation and confirmation in our personal lives is invaluable. Before arriving at Victory World Church, Montell had been the minister of music at a different church for seven years. I had served in accounting and all our chil-dren served somewhere in the ministry as well. When the Lord released us to leave that church and we first came to Victory, we tried to steer far away from the music department and the other areas where we had previously served. After hearing a message on family, serving and volunteering, followed by a plea for volunteers from the senior pastor, Dennis Rouse, only a week or two into our visits, we immediately began serving in the children's department and intentionally determined to stay off the music and leadership radars completely.

Eight months into serving the children, one of the young adult worship pastors approached us and asked my husband if he would consider joining a special service of praise and worship with them on an upcoming weekend. We discussed this amongst ourselves, then reluctantly conceded and said we would do it. There had been talks around the church about how talented Montell was, how well he could sing, how anointed he was; however, we were still apprehensive because of our music business past.

That Sunday came and my husband sang to the glory of the Lord. I can remember watching it and I couldn't contain the joy that I felt inside. Following years of performing on stages, my husband was returning to the gifting of his youth, his calling, and I now watched him on the platform in a position of influence as he led the people in worship. I can recall saying, "This is what he was born to do." As he finished praise and worship, you could see how liberated and free he felt, and I saw him come alive like never before. In an unusual moment immediately following worship, our senior pastor got up and said, "Brother, I don't know where you came from...but that was praise and worship!" This was huge for many reasons.

The other leaders and people had been encouraging and telling my husband (or affirming) who he was, but the *confirmation* of who my husband was came from our pastor. Following all the affirmations, the deal was sealed when the words came from the authority that had been placed over our lives to confirm identity. In each of these instances, where God confirmed the Son-ship of Jesus following His baptismal, where Jesus confirmed Peter was on track because only the Father could have revealed the correct answers to him, or when our spiritual covering, Pastor Dennis confirmed Montell was a worship leader before he was a worship leader, the constant theme is that the confirmation comes from the authority over our lives. Confirmation is the seal or stamp of approval. Confirmation activates the affirmations spoken over our lives, enabling us to walk in our destiny.

Let's now examine how this principle of confirmation is applicable to marriage. We should understand the power of the words we speak over our spouses, as they are extremely powerful. Scripture reminds us in Proverbs 18:21 that the words we say hold life and death. So, what are we speaking over our spouses? Are we declaring life or death over our soul mates?

Maybe you are at an impasse in your marriage or at a crossroads where trial and test intersect. Regardless of what season you're in, you will undoubtedly have the opportunity to choose how you use your words in the midst of a difficult situation. Things are not always what they appear to be, so we don't want to be deceived by what we see with our natural eyes. Even though that situation or circumstance may look messy, hurtful, unforgivable and unbearable, the way you speak life or death into that situation will determine your graceful or not so graceful emergence from that life experience.

Years ago, we walked through a season when my husband's music career was on the decline and he was in a lull and becoming more frustrated and depressed daily. He had experienced losing a recording contract, we were having marital issues, and he wasn't working like he had in the past. This led to financial strain, pressure, lack of self-esteem and many other issues. This cycle went on for quite a while. I could have looked at that situation and harped on the obvious issues or I could choose to do something else. Please understand I didn't see this difficult season coming to an end; in fact, it did not appear as if the end was near at all. Everything about how it looked in the physical was dismal, to say the least, yet I was praying and asking God to reveal in the spirit how to navigate these waters because with my natural eye, no relief was in sight.

He answered and instructed me to read Romans chapter 4. In this scripture, he reminded me of the father of our faith, Abraham, and how he believed even when he did not see the promise yet. Basically, Abraham was honored because although he could not see, he moved forward in total faith. In spite of what he could see, he still chose to believe God. Verse 17 of that chapter says *he called those things that were not as though they were.* I really had to wrap my mind around this. Abraham was very old and he was called the father of many nations. He and his wife were way too old to be having children, and yet, Isaac was born. Abraham chose faith over the facts.

God challenged me do the same thing He had asked of Abraham, to *call those things which were not as though they were.* So that's what I began to do. I began to affirm the character of my husband. I told Montell he was a great father, a great husband, a great provider, a tremendous man of God and a valiant warrior, and that people would rise up and call him blessed. Everything he touched was blessed and people would give him favor everywhere he went. Day after day, month after month I would confess these things over him and to him. God had given me the seed, yet the word had to water it. And over time, God made that seed grow into exactly what I confessed all throughout that word-planting season. It was not instant, but it is absolutely true that every word I confessed was a seed planted with an expected harvest. I sent out my words to accomplish what I needed them to and they did exactly that. I declared all the things my husband was, even when he wasn't, and then God the Father came along and confirmed those declarations and affirmations as truth. We normally have to see it to believe it, yet exercising faith requires us to believe it to see it.

There is something miraculous about the power in a father's approval. We all can use our words to water the gifts that the Lord has given us to call greatness into existence. Presenting extensive resumes, recalling past accomplishments and relishing human approval from men is not enough. Like the title of an old TV program, "Father Knows Best." The word works, but you must work it.

Here's another more personal example. All my life, I've had the desire to be thin. I have always battled with weight loss and gain, and it has been a struggle for me my entire life. When my husband and I got married he became a very prominent, highly visible and successful man. In the glamorous world of the music industry, many (if not most) of the wives are a size four to six or smaller. It was very difficult to not judge and compare myself to the other industry wives. My husband knew my struggle, and he could have taken the stance of, "Why can't you look like the other wives?" Instead, he would say, "Babe, you look so beautiful. I love you just the way you are, and you are the woman I have always dreamed of. There is no one I think about or desire but you."

Regardless of what I actually weighed, he was speaking *to my future*. As I write this many years later, following the raising of four children, I am currently only 10 pounds shy of my ideal lifetime weight goal! While I continue to work for my goal, the reality is that Zumba at 4:30am each morning, personal fitness trainers, tasteless foods and the consumption of more than a gallon of water each day (including innumerable restroom visits) only supplement the *word* that was planted on the inside. I now feel beautiful and healthy on the outside, but his words watered my soul on the inside. He affirmed who I was before I was. Then my Father in Heaven confirmed the truths that were spoken over my life and produced the harvest of me becoming the healthiest me I could possibly be. My husband now hashtags me on social media with #hotwife=good-life. Words matter. They become the seed. Your spouse's heart is the soil. What are you planting and expecting to grow? What you put into it, you will get out of it.

Sometimes it truly is difficult to speak positive affirmations in negative situations. However, the truth is that in the darkest and most grotesque places in our lives, we can be the tools that provide the godly affirmation He seeks to confirm. God may use us to profess that our spouse is healthy, rich, kind, a great parent, a great spouse, a successful businessperson and we can fill in the blank. Society instructs us to call it as we see it; Jesus equips us to call it before we see it. God can use us to be the words and voice of reason that gives our spouse the strength to not give up.

God created the whole world using His words. He didn't do an abracadabra, hocus-pocus hand gesture to bring the universe into existence, nor did He have any sparkly dust or magic beans to create the world. He just *spoke* the words and the earth and everything in it was formed. We were created in His image and we have the power and the authority to do the same things. The question is: What have we been using our words to do? Have our words accomplished exactly what we have sent them to do?

[MJ & KJ] The challenge for us all is to speak life and not death, in spite of what we see. There is greatness inside each and every one of us, given by God. It will be affirmed by us as spouses and spoken as seeds in a field. The washing and watering of the word and our prayers will fertilize it and, in its due season, God will come along and confirm that which you have spoken over your spouse's life. *Speak what you desire to reap.* Words of affirmation create a more bountiful harvest. Whatever you plant will grow! What are you planting? Our mom says, "You can't plant peas and get corn." If you are planting words of discord, that's what you will get. If you are planting words of blessing, that's what you will get. If you don't have positive words of your own to speak, affirm what God's word says. Familiarize yourself with His promises and what He says in the word about your spouse and mentally put it on repeat. In due season, God can confirm it and you will watch it come to pass.

We have provided some Confessions for both husbands and wives to speak over each other daily. These are truths to affirm over one another as God begins to confirm and birth our words into reality. We pray you allow your Father in Heaven to confirm these affirmations over you.

Daily Confessions for a Husband over His Wife

Joshua 24:15

As for me and my house we will serve The Lord.

Proverbs 3:3

Love and Faithfulness never leave me; I bind them around my neck. I write them on the tablet of my heart.

Ecclesiastes 9:9

I will live joyfully with the wife whom I love all the days of my life, which He has given me under the sun.

Mark 10:6-9

From the beginning of creation God made male and female. For this reason I have left behind my father and mother (and other family) and am joined to my wife and cleave closely to her permanently, and we two have become one flesh, so that we are no longer two, but one flesh. What therefore God has united (joined together), no man will separate or divide.

Ephesians 4:31-32

I am not mean, bad tempered and angry. I will not quarrel and say harsh words. These things should have no place in my life. I am kind to my wife, tenderhearted, forgiving, just as God has forgiven me because I belong to Christ.

Ephesians 5:25-28

I show the same kind of love to my wife as Christ showed to the church when He died for her, to make her holy and clean, washed by Baptism and God's word; so that He could give her to Himself as a glorious church without a single wrinkle or any other blemish, being holy and without a single fault. This is how husbands should treat their wives, loving them as parts of themselves. For since a man and his wife are now one, a man is really doing himself a favor and loving himself when he loves his wife!

Colossians 3:8-10, 12-14

I put away and rid myself (completely) of all these things: anger, rage, bad feelings toward my wife, curses and slander, and foul-mouthed abuse and shameful utterances from my lips! I do not lie, for I have stripped off the old self with its evil practices, and have clothed myself as God's own chosen one...who is purified and holy and well-beloved by God Himself, by putting on tenderhearted pity and mercy, a lowly opinion of myself, gentle ways, and patience. I am gentle and forbearing, readily pardoning others; even as the Lord has forgiven me. Above all these things I put on love and enfold myself with my wife with the bond of perfectness (which binds everything together completely in ideal harmony).

James 5:16

I confess my faults to my wife, and we pray for one another, that we may be healed. The effectual fervent prayer of the righteous man avails much.

1 Peter 3:7

I give honor to my wife, and I treat her with understanding as we live together. She may be weaker than I am, but she is my equal partner in God's gift of new life. If I don't treat her as I should, my prayers will not be heard.

Men, we challenge you to actually pray these confessions aloud as declarations covering your wife. Allow her to hear you speak these words of life over her.

Daily Confessions for a Wife over Her Husband

Proverbs 12:4

An excellent wife is the crown of her husband. I am an excellent wife.

Proverbs 31:10-12

I am a wife of noble character, I am worth far more than rubies. My husband has full confidence in me and lacks nothing of value, I bring him good, not harm, all the days of my life.

Proverbs 31:26

I open my mouth with skillful and godly wisdom and on my tongue is the law of kindness (giving counsel and instruction).

1 Corinthians 13:1-8

I operate in the spiritual gifts toward my husband. Love is patient; I am patient. Love is kind; I am kind. Love does not envy; I do not envy. Love does not boast, it is not proud. I do not boast, I am not proud. Love is not rude, self-seeking or easily angered, it keeps no record of wrong. I am not rude, self-seeking, or easily angered. I keep no record of wrongs. Love does not delight in evil, but rejoices in the truth. I do not delight in evil, but rejoice with the truth. Love always protects, always trusts, always hopes, always perseveres. Love never fails. I always protect, always trust, always hope, always persevere.

Ephesians 5:33

I respect and reverence my husband. I notice him, regard him, honor him, prefer him, venerate him, and esteem him. I defer to him, praise him, love and admire him exceedingly.

1 Thessalonians 5:11, 15-18

I encourage my husband and build him up. I do not pay back wrong for wrong, but always try to be kind to him. I am joyful always. I pray continually; giving thanks in all circumstances, for this is God's will for me in Christ Jesus.

1 Timothy 3:11

I am worthy of respect and serious, not a gossiper but temperate and self-controlled, (thoroughly) trustworthy in all things.

1 Peter 3:1-5

I am submissive to my husband so that he may be won over without words, but by my behavior, when he sees the purity and reverence of my life. I have the unfading beauty of a gentle and quiet spirit, which is of great worth in God's sight. This is the way that the Holy women of the past who put their hope in God used to make themselves beautiful.

1 John 3:18

I love not merely in theory or in speech, but in deed and in truth and practice and its sincerity.

Women, we challenge you to actually pray these confessions aloud as declarations covering your husband. Allow him to hear you speak these words of life over him. Our marriage has elevated beyond belief by speaking these words of life over one another.

What we affirm, the Father confirms. This is also a great practice for those who one day desire to be married. Begin speaking these confessions over your spouse to declare blessing over them even prior to marriage.

CHAPTER 9

Moving From the Me Train to the We Train

[MJ & KJ] If you think life moves fast, consider marriage a nitrogen pack strapped to husbands and wives to thrust us into our destiny. A huge transition takes place when two singles unite to become a single *unit*. This is the journey from "me" to "we." This transformation can prove challenging, as many of us were trained by our parents to become individuals who can make it in this world on our own. In reality, we are selfish by nature, and from birth we are catered to until we are able to care for ourselves. We are reminded of watching Joyce Meyer jokingly recite in a repetitive robotic voice, "What about me? What about me? What about me?"

Self-preservation is the first law of human nature, yet Christ executed the greatest act of love in the history of mankind by laying down His life for all. This is an example of how different our thoughts and ways are from the one who created us. Most of us are seeking to preserve our lives when scripture instructs us that we must be willing to lose our lives in order to gain them for eternity. As Jesus lived by example to give His life for all, we are asked to lay down our lives for our spouses, placing the wants, needs and desires of another over our own. Marriage mirrors how the Father, Son and Holy Spirit work together in harmonious unity within our lives here on earth. Symbolically, it is a beautiful exchange where we find greater purpose in life as we become more like Christ. If we have been traveling down "Me Blvd" and the street sign ahead suddenly changes to "We Parkway," some things need to change. Not so much our direction, but more importantly, our thinking! No more *De La Soul*; No longer is it about "Me, Myself and I." There is a new trio that will have to emerge in order for you to succeed--God, your spouse and you. The quicker this transition is made, the better. Yes, life indeed moves fast -- so get ready!

We often liken the journey from "me" to "we" to a five-stop train ride. Understand that once the marital train is moving, you don't get off until you reach your final destination. The train may take several different paths to reach the desired ending point, yet the most direct path is often the least chosen. Sometimes we think we may have boarded the wrong train. We are not talking about marrying the wrong person, but rather finding ourselves again going the "me" direction instead of "we," which may result in layovers, delays and long and uncomfortable traveling conditions. Train hopping is not allowed; therefore, it is a good idea to know where you're going prior to leaving the station. We submit that there are five stops on the journey from "me" to "we:"

1. Submission
2. Sequence
3. Sold Out
4. Sacrifice
5. Serving

There will be more stops ahead, but these five will definitely get us on the right track as we build our foundation. On the route from self-sufficient and independent to all-sufficient and interdependent, these rest areas give us a map to guide us from our selfishness to a selfless destination. Whatever ideals have been planted inside us from parents, dating, friends, entertainment and anything else we can think of regarding marriage may need to be reconsidered once we include these plans into the blueprint. In context of the blueprint, consider these the five things a building inspector will need to review and approve before signing off to permit further godly marital construction. We will spend the most time on submission, as this may require the most renovation.

1. Submission

[KJ] When I was a little girl, my mom taught me to be self-sufficient and independent. She did this because this was not taught to her as a little girl, and she felt like she wished she had been taught this. So I was taught not to rely on anyone else and that I was the driving force behind becoming successful. My mom loved me and desired more for me. In preparation for many of the challenges in life she experienced herself, I believe this parental ideology was birthed from damaged self-esteem, value and her feelings of unworthiness stripped from her during the course of three marriages. Mom imparted strength into me and embedded in me a mindset to depend on no one but myself. She taught me to not settle for less than I deserved or was capable of because I held my own keys to my future. My future did not lie in a man, but in how driven I was to be successful. I know she meant these things to propel me forward, and it did; however, these thoughts were very much engrained in my psyche.

You know those little girls who dream of one day marrying a handsome prince charming, wearing a white wedding gown down to the alter followed by a lifetime of happiness living in a house surrounded by a white picket fence, 2.5 kids and a dog? Well, I believed I would grow up to own the million dollar company *that might hire that girl to work for me*. My picture of marriage was not painted in bright colors. Mom raised me and imparted a confidence in me to succeed in college and to strive for success in my career. Later in life, though, I would find these thoughts are totally counterproductive to success in a godly marriage.

When I first met Montell, I was totally smitten by him and although I never thought I would get married, I somehow could see myself marrying him. Even while falling in love, I knew I wanted to be successful and independent, which in my mind meant I didn't need to be married or have children. My goal was to become a successful businesswoman and make a name for myself. Reaching that mark equated success, according to my training.

My ideas about marriage and career aspirations soon began to collide. These thoughts seemed to conflict with each other, and I found myself at a crossroads. Finally surrendering to love, I decided that I was going to concede to doing the "marriage thing," yet I remained firm on not doing the "kid thing." Even though I had changed my mind in regard to marriage, I was unwilling to change my mind about my quest to make a name for myself.

For example, when we first got married I did not change my name. Instead, I hyphenated my last name trying to hold on to a part of my *old identity* so that people would see me still as myself, as if it were a bad thing to be married and accepting my husband's name and covering. In the industry we were in, being married and having a family was looked upon as weak and a setback, so I was determined not to let that happen to me. I allowed my prior programming and my quest for success to affect the foundation of my marriage. In essence, by not changing my name I was rejecting my covering. I was unaware at the time, but not fully accepting my husband's name also planted a seed that I was not accepting a part of him. I rejected part of my inheritance or blessing of the covenant.

It was that "me" thinking that would cost us the first seven years of our marriage. It allowed us to make decisions that would almost secure our demise. Keeping my dad's name to honor him seemed like a small and harmless gesture at the time, but the violation of so many godly principles for my own advancement would lead us both down dangerous paths. I was taught to be strong in the natural, where the word says that in my weakness, He is made strong. *Violation*. I was determined to keep my old name, yet the word instructed me that in Christ, I was a new creation. *Violation*. The reality is simply this: by not completely taking on my husband's name, identity and covering, *I felt like there was a part of me that did not have to submit to him.*

Although this is not always the case for keeping one's maiden name, I would submit that 99.9% of the time it is absolutely the case. If we don't accept who we've become, we will always revert to what we know: old thoughts, old patterns and old ways. Name change was a big deal to God in scripture as it dealt directly with *identity*. For example, Abram became Abraham, and Sarai became Sara; the new name given was always about what that person was to become! Jacob wrestled with God all night long and after prevailing, God changed his name from Jacob (meaning trickster) to Israel (fought with God and man and won). There is power in accepting the new name. Ironically, one of the keys I would learn from not changing my name was that in my lack of submission, I had opened the door for the enemy to run amuck on my marriage. I had always looked at the "S" word (submission) almost as a curse word. I would later find out was there is power in submission. This is the key principle we must grab a hold of as the first lesson of becoming "we."

> *"Submit to one another in the fear of God. Wives, submit to your own husbands, as to the Lord. For the husband is head of the wife, as also Christ is head of the church; and He is the Savior of the body. Therefore, just as the church is subject to Christ, so let the wives be to their own husbands in everything." Ephesians 5:21-24 (NKJV)*

Sub·mis·sion: a willingness to yield or surrender to somebody, or the act of doing so.

[MJ] The word *submission* has really gotten a bad rap. It's been looked upon as a show of weakness when, in reality, it is a sign of strength. One of the ways submission is best demonstrated is within the world of wrestling.

I have to say, I've always been a WWE fan. I've had seasons when I would watch wrestling all the time and then seasons when I hardly watched a match. However, even when I wasn't keeping up with the sport, I would often be flipping through the channels, see a match and get sucked right back in. Regardless of your opinion about wrestling, there still is an undeniable reality involved in this sport. Whether for professional entertainment or high school, college or Olympic sports, the athletes all understand this rule of wrestling: *the submission hold wins.*

Two opponents are battling to pin one another. One of the wrestlers gets the other in what is commonly known as a "submission hold." This is an extremely uncomfortable position to be in. It can also be embarrassing to find oneself in this compromising position and what's worse is that there is no escape from a submission hold. In order to advance and be freed from this hold, one of two things must happen; either the person in the compromised position must submit by "tapping out," or something is going to *break.* Please understand the hold is not designed to break the opponent but to bring about a release from the compromising and uncomfortable and potentially hazardous situation. Nothing actually has to be broken to be released, except maybe the opponent's pride.

This can also be applied in our marriages. If one spouse does not want to submit to the other, it may result in something being broken, namely hearts and possibly even the marriage itself. We clearly understand that submission is not something we like to do; if we wanted to submit, that would be called agreement, not submission. Submitting actually means *to defer to someone else's authority*. Unlike wrestling, submission in marriage is not to get the upper hand over our spouse, but rather to defer or prefer our spouse to our own agendas. A willingness to surrender to someone else in the context of a marriage is a beautiful thing. Trust that God has placed you with the one He designed to complement your soul during your earthly lifetime.

To view submission to our spouse as honoring to God is spiritually mature thinking. And for the wives reading this, prayerfully seek to submit to your husband the same way you would like to see him submitted to God. I have found women don't mind submitting to a man who is completely submitted to Christ. There is safety in submission. There is safety in surrender. There is safety in serving. God sent him to you, so He will also teach him how to nurture and take care of that which has been placed in his care, namely you. Further in Ephesians chapter 5, valuable instruction is shared regarding marriage and is a great meditation and practice in submitting to our spouses. Wives, you are called to submit to your husbands as unto the Lord; husbands, we are called to die to ourselves, love our wives and give our lives for them, just as Christ did for the church. Ladies, clearly you get the better end of the deal on this one. Welcome to the first stop on the journey from "me" to "we."

2. Sequence

[MJ & KJ] The second thing we should do on this journey from "me" to "we" is stay true to "first things first." We have two number ones; a number one in Heaven and a number one on earth. We must make the main thing the main thing.

Our first love in Heaven is the Lord. First and foremost, we must keep Him in our mind and prioritize Him with our time and focus. If we seek Him first, the rest of the things in our lives can flow smoothly. We cannot have an intimate relationship with someone we don't spend quality time with, correct? Intimacy shouldn't be rushed. If we do not spend quality time in prayer and the word, our foundation will be shaky.

Our other number one on earth is our spouse. In this same manner of establishing priorities, there must be quality time spent for authentic relational intimacy. If we don't make the effort to spend time with our spouse, our foundation will also be shaky. Let's make sure our number ones here on earth are first on our list. Here again is the friendly reminder: God, spouse, children, church, family and friends, career, everything else. What we do does not determine who we are, but who we are *does* determine what we do. Focusing more on our spouse than ourselves creates an atmosphere of "we." A husband and wife submitting to each other and making each other a priority is the perfect image of a "we" mentality.

[MJ] Sequence places an emphasis on order. Anything that is out of sequence is out of order. For example, I have spoken with men who have difficulty with something as simple as placing the toilet seat down in the restroom. There are tons of messages a toilet seat left up can send. It says we are selfish. It says, "You're not worth the effort of me using the muscle strength required to complete this task." It says, "You are not worth remembering." It says, "Do it yourself." I could go on and on. However, something as simple as putting the seat down says, "In our home, our kingdom, you are the queen and I value you enough to *always* have your seat prepared." This may seem silly, but it should also seem selfless. This is a part of "we" thinking. "We" thinking sets the atmosphere in our relationship. We can set the comfortable and desired climate of our homes -- the temperature of our marriage -- and our spouses are the thermostats. They may be turned off, turned on or turned up! Make sure everything is in proper working order. Oh yeah, and keep the seat *down*. Welcome to our second stop.

3. Sold Out

[MJ & KJ] Thirdly, on the journey from "me" to "we," we have to learn how we must enter into this partnership. We have always heard about each person in a relationship bringing an equal 50% to the table. We submit to you that in a godly, full 50/50 partnership, both spouses need to bring their 100% to the relationship. Each person bringing only 50% would mean they were half in and half out, which will not work. When we hear someone describe that they are going to give their best, they will often describe it as giving 110%. Why would we give 110% effort, blood, sweat and tears to a job or hobby yet only bring 50% into our marriage?

What would marriage look like if both spouses brought 110%? It's simple God math. This 220% partnership begins to take a different shape, doesn't it?

[KJ] It is also important to remember that no one dominates in an equal partnership. When someone is dominating another, they are controlling or lording over the other. This kind of behavior is counterproductive to the design of marriage. Control implies being forced to or the taking of something; these are not terms that should be exercised in the context of marriage. Where dominance is present, there is an absence of peace. Dominance and peace cannot coexist. They are on opposite spectrums. The very meaning of peace is the absence of hostility. Peace is critical to a productive, happy, and healthy home environment. When you maintain a peaceful environment in your home, it will create a healthy culture where the seed of "we" flourishes. Being sold out means bringing your 110% to the table, not taking 110% from it. Welcome to our third stop. Are you still with us? All aboard!

4. Sacrifice

[MJ & KJ] The fourth stop on the "me" to "we" train is sacrifice. Sacrifice is an easier concept to grasp than submission yet also very counter-culture in the "all about me" world we live in. This idea of sacrifice is also easier said than done. Sacrifice means *the forfeiture of something highly valued for the sake of one considered to have a greater value or claim.* Sacrificing ourselves for the greater potential of who we are as a unit is something that is not only honorable, but a building block in creating a successful marriage. The ability to unselfishly put our spouse's needs above our own is an art. It is something beautiful to behold and unique to each husband and wife's interpretation of how to exercise this gift. Practicing this is not only a challenge when it is just the two of you, but it intensifies when children are added in the equation.

Our entire belief system is built on sacrifice; God gave His only begotten Son as a sacrifice so that we would have eternal life. Throughout scripture, God repeatedly references this exchange as a marriage. Because God sacrificed for us, we will have to sacrifice as well, in order to resemble our Father. To carry Christ's DNA, we forfeit ourselves for the sake of our spouse. This is the time when we look most like our Dad.

To sacrifice requires faith. This is a faith that what we are giving up for another will be for our good, as well as the good of the one for whom we are sacrificing. Many times a husband or a wife will feel as though they are making a great sacrifice for their spouse and receiving nothing in return. The action has the characteristics of sacrifice when, in actuality, they are positioning themselves to be a martyr. God never required us to be martyrs in marriage. Thankfully, physical death is not required or even asked of us in sacrifice. However, we *are* asked to die to our fleshly desires so that we may be likened to the one in whom we place our faith. In sacrificing our "me" for the "we," we produce a better quality of life promised to us by the one who modeled the ultimate sacrifice. What are we willing to give up? Are we willing to sacrifice without expecting anything in return? One more stop ahead.

5. Serving

[KJ] The final stop on this journey from "me" to "we" requires that we learn the value of serving our spouse. If we value something, we take care of it and treat it much differently than something we think of as disposable. Many times we take better care of our car, clothes, shoes, homes and material possessions than we do our spouse. All of these things are temporal and have no eternal value, and yet we have a tendency to treat them with more care. We wash, clean, maintain, mend and pour into and even take out insurance on these earthly material possessions.

I wonder what would happen if we poured that same effort into our most significant relationship outside of God? Quite possibly an overflow; our spouse would feel protected, valued, bright, covered, tended to, and full. This sounds like a recipe for a happy marriage. Let's take a moment to think of how we have been investing our time, energy, affections and effort into our spouse. Have we placed greater value on material things of this world or the greatest earthly gift God has given us?

[MJ] Kristin and I have made it a point to try and out-serve each other. This is an activity where no one in our home loses. Serving each other makes us constantly aware of our spouse's presence in our lives, as well as the presence of God holding us together.

We serve each other as parents. Even when tired following a long ministry Tuesday filled with meetings about meetings, I will volunteer to take my son to school early the next morning even though my wife may have it covered. I do this because I want to serve her. I am also serving my son, who loves for me to take him to school because it shows him that I value him more than I value an extra hour of sleep. Ultimately, it becomes self-serving because I probably get blessed more than they do by doing it. We serve our kids.

We also serve together in marriage ministry. I have said that although I enjoy speaking and teaching, I often feel strongest when Kristin and I have the opportunity to do ministry together. Seeing me is only experiencing ½ the story. Seeing us both in action is the only way to really comprehend how dynamic God is and has been in our lives. The couples we have counseled for marriage ministry understand what this looks and feels like. We serve the ministry.

We also serve each other intimately. We had a newborn in my mid 40's... so enough said about that! We serve each other and challenge each other by making this a regular practice.

One of my all time favorite soul groups, The Mighty OJays, had a song called the "Love Train." Whether you are just starting out at the station or you have been steamrolling ahead for some time, we challenge you to get on this train. We can all get on board and take the five stops necessary to a better marriage.

"Me" to "we" is a transformation. Your language will begin to change. Instead of "I" did this and "she" did that, you will begin to notice you are discussing what "we" did and what "we" are doing and the wonderful plans involving what "we" are going to do. Change your mind and your heart will follow. Let's think submission, sequence, sold out, sacrifice and service. These "S" words *will* change our minds and eventually, our marriages. Whatsoever a man or woman thinks, they become.

CHAPTER 10

What Language Does Your Heart Speak?

[MJ & KJ] Grasping this next communication concept could change your lives forever, as it did ours.

[KJ] Funny, late one night, I was flipping through different Christian TV channels (not that watching Christian television is funny or anything, but it was funny that I was up late) when I happened to stumble upon Joyce Meyer having a conversation with an interesting gentleman. I enjoy Joyce's ministry, so I lingered there for a moment and quickly got sucked into what they were saying. The man in the conversation was Gary Chapman, author of the best seller, *The 5 Love Languages: The Secret to Love That Lasts*. Their dialogue had me mesmerized. He presented something that seemed so simple yet profound, and I was hearing it for the very first time.

He went on to say that every person's love language is different. He submitted that if we don't find out the love languages of the people around us, we are living less than a full life. What? My husband and children have their own love languages? I have a love language? My mind began spinning.

That night a light went on in my head that changed the way I thought about my spouse and my children forever. I became concerned at the notion that I might have been ineffective at loving my family or at the very least, in loving them the way they desired to be loved. I was trying to love them the way I love. I did not understand that the way I loved them, in fact, did not love any of them at all. How could that even be possible? I cooked, cleaned, ran errands, taxied kids like super shuttle, attended all the games, made all the meetings...I served them with everything within me, and yet I'm not loving them??? I was frustrated at even the thought of them having the nerve to say that they didn't feel loved. I had not only been giving them my love, but also every effort and moment of time I had and yet they somehow feel unloved? I needed clarification and revelation to comprehend how this was possible.

Gary went on to describe that there are five primary love languages. He suggested that when we understand that how we love and how others around us love is probably different -- almost like speaking a different language -- communication can be translated and open up our lives to a whole new type of love. In essence, we could revolutionize our love lives by learning to speak the language of those around us we love.

The five primary love languages:

1. **Physical Touch**: It's all about the appropriate physical touch.

2. **Quality Time**: To show love is to give your undivided attention and focus.

3. **Gifts**: For some people, what makes them feel most loved is to receive a gift.

4. **Words of Affirmation**: This language uses the power of words to affirm other people.

5. **Acts of Service**: For these people, action speaks louder than words.

What I quickly figured out after listening to his explanations and going to his website to take the quick profile test (www.5love-languages.com) is that my personal love language is *acts of service.* In my efforts to love my family, I was doing and doing and doing. I was relentless in showing them through serving how much I loved them, never understanding why I was missing the mark.

After taking the test, I found out that each person in my family had a love language different from my own.

My husband's love language is *quality time*. During those times when I was with him yet multitasking to try and get everything done, I was actually saying to him that he was not important and that I did not love him. My attention was divided. To speak his love language, I actually learned how to put down my phone, put down my to-do list and my multitasking abilities and sit still in his presence. To my surprise, we don't have to be doing anything or even saying anything; just being together is enough for him and speaks volumes of my love to him. If I can be transparent, this was very difficult for me to do. It took intense effort to learn how to slow down and just be with my husband. Nothing shows value to a time person like actually being there when you're there. The other love languages work for this person at some level as well but if the primary mark is missed, those others can still cause the recipient to feel unloved.

My oldest son Christopher's love language is *gifts*. Yikes! I spent years prior to learning this love language information showing a love that couldn't be seen. I had been speaking my language of love to him with no interpreter. So while I'm running him around to events and washing clothes and making dinner, loving him (or so I thought), he was just waiting to get to his birthday and Christmas so he could feel loved. Wow! The reverse of this is also true. He would jump through hoops to try and save money to purchase me a bracelet or necklace for a Mother's Day gift when I would've felt more appreciated with a handwritten card. A hand-painted picture or a home-cooked breakfast that showed an act of service would have meant the world! To a gifts person, nothing shows more value and love than receiving a gift. People most often show love the way they desire to receive it. A giver normally shows how they value you by giving; at the same time, they feel loved when they receive gifts and may feel neglected in the absence of them.

My oldest daughter Sydney is a combination of *time* and *touch*, so while I was again completing my to-do list at the end of the night preparing for the activities of the next day during her snuggle time, I was saying "I don't value you." She certainly wasn't feeling important as I neglected both time and closeness. This is extremely important in regards to our spouse and children; if a love need is not being met, we humanly seek to fulfill this missing desire in other places. The enemy may then seek to pervert a simple need or desire to become sin. Lack of a mother's or father's touch may then be communicated from an admiring friend or relative and possibly open the door to inappropriate touch, time and attention being sought after. Sadly, authentic love can become replaced with counterfeit affection. It is important to display the original love sought after by our loved ones so when the fake presents itself, they recognize it. Real love recognizes real love.

My youngest son Skyler's love language is *words of affirmation*. So when I was getting frustrated because all the things I was doing went unnoticed, I was barking at him and watching his whole countenance change because of the way I conveyed my message in frustration. My words had greater effect over him than any of the other four languages I could speak. Montell and I are careful when correcting him because what we say and how we say it translates differently to him. Nothing shows love to a words of affirmation person more than speaking life and appreciation into their spirit.

My youngest daughter Samantha's love language is also *touch*. Even at a young age, we may begin to identify what communicates love to the ones closest to us. I recall one day she just couldn't seem to wait for me to pick her up and hold her, and I waited because I had just one more load of laundry to do. There's a difference between being spoiled and being neglected. She pitched a mini-fit until I held her and all was again right in the world.

Once I was opened to the world of these five languages, I realized I was unintentionally missing the mark with every single one of my children. I love and value my husband and my family, yet none of them felt loved at all. Although this could not be further from the truth, you don't know what you don't know.

Once I figured out how to love them, it made things so much simpler and easier to hit the mark. It's easier to hit a target you can see. I stopped with my furious "to do" lists and began rearranging my time and efforts to show each of them in their own love language just how much they were loved and appreciated. I can't tell you that it was instant and that I don't occasionally still miss the mark, but I can tell you that this was a game changer for me. Loving in their language cut down on the frustration, anger, anxiety and fussing in our home. I began communicating love in a way they could receive it, and this also released me to feel valued for my efforts. It created an atmosphere of love and appreciation and caused my house to become a house of peace, where love abounds.

[MJ] I can also testify that speaking the wrong language, even with the right motive, can prove unproductive. I think back to one holiday in particular during my R&B days and I was proactively going Christmas shopping for a gift for Kristin about 48 hours before Christmas. I found myself at an expensive clothing store where I began looking at the furs. There was a mink shawl that was absolutely gorgeous and cost about $4k. I then spotted a full-length mink coat that cost around $16k. In my "man mind," I imagined giving my wife the first smaller coat as a decoy and then surprising her with the full-length as the real gift. Bam! So I put this plan into action and I can recall executing this presentation of my love and affection just as I imagined it. However, it didn't really go over as I expected. She was gracious and appreciative in her reaction, but something was missing. I was attempting to speak the language of purchases and materials and possessions and gifts to an *acts of service* person. I learned an expensive lesson that Christmas. I only wish I could have learned of Dr. Chapman's resources sooner. Save yourself some money, heartache and possibly a chinchilla if your spouse's love language isn't gifts.

It's never too late to begin learning a new language. Around year fifteen of our marriage, Kristin said she wanted to share with me one of her biggest pet peeves. *Biggest pet peeves*? What could possibly be that big after fifteen years of marriage? What could be so big that couldn't have been brought up, well, let's just say, maybe fifteen years prior? She began to tell me that she hates that I never make up the bed. She had a point. In fifteen years of being married, I could not remember once making a conscious effort to make the bed. She then told me that leaving the bed disheveled and returning to it the same way in the evening made her want to return to it less. She confided that one of her enjoyments of staying at a hotel is leaving the room to return to a freshly made bed. For her, there is just something about a freshly made bed. It made her want to get in it. I repeat, returning home to a freshly made bed made her desire to get into it. You had better believe I began to make the bed.

I had to learn to speak her *acts of service* love language. I began doing it and when she would notice, she made efforts to say and show that she appreciated it. The funny thing that happened is that now I make the bed whether she notices or not. Whether she notices or not, I don't make the bed to elicit a response; I make the bed to love her. I stopped loving her how I wanted to love her, or how I desire to be loved, and sought to serve her. The result is a vibrant and active intimate life and the addition of a new baby midway into our 40s. What's the point of this exercise? Men, make the bed.

If your spouse is *acts of service*, make the bed. Do the dishes. Vacuum the carpet. Study her language and cherish the fact that we never stop learning. This means things can always be fresh and new. We receive the benefits of our return on investment. Make the bed. (I'm gonna put this subject to bed now... a freshly made bed, that you can bet!)

One day Kristin had the car filled with gas and took it to the car wash. I had personally taken the car to have it washed just two days prior and didn't think it was dirty and therefore, didn't notice it had been washed again. As we are driving around that day, I noticed she was visibly upset. When I asked her if I did something wrong, she asked, "Did you notice that I had the car cleaned?"

Like a novice I replied, "Oh, I just had the car cleaned two days ago." It was not Christmas when this happened, although it quickly became *a very silent night.* I didn't recognize her attempt to love me because she was speaking in her *acts of service* dialect and she didn't understand I was frustrated that she showed up thirty minutes late to the airport, cutting into the amount of *time* that we were supposed to spend together that day. We often found ourselves speaking a foreign language to each other, wondering why we couldn't hear one another. Life comes with no subtitles, so it's important to recognize that just because our spouses don't hear us, doesn't mean they aren't listening.

Have you ever heard the popular saying, "Time is money"? Well, I rephrased that to say, "Time is more than money." Money comes and goes. We can lose money and get it back, but not time. Once it's gone, it's gone. Thankfully, however, God can redeem what was lost.

As my wife mentioned earlier, she is a champion at multi-tasking. We would be going somewhere in the car and as I drove her around she would be texting, checking email, making calls, surfing the web and seemingly doing everything outside of me. I would become extremely frustrated, not so much from her actions, but more so because she couldn't see or recognize what she was doing. Sometimes spouses desire to be loved without having to say they need to be loved. In my instance, it wasn't what she said but what she didn't say. Her nonverbal communication said to me that I was not important. I also had to understand that she couldn't read my mind and the same way she shared a pet peeve 15 years into the marriage, I brought one of my own to the table. I shared with her that when she was with me, I wanted her to be present. This was not easy for her.

Once she was aware that being with me only required her to actually be with me, she began to be intentional. She would fight to not pick up the phone or read a text. She would eventually find that she didn't even have to say anything to simply be present. Today, we can sit together in a room and there is no uncomfortable silence. The T.V. or radio doesn't even have to be on. We can talk, say anything or say nothing. Her silent action screamed unspoken love. Even in silence, she says she loves me by speaking my love language of *time*.

[MJ & KJ] Perhaps you'd like to learn the love languages of you and your spouse. The information we are presenting in this blueprint can be accessed at www.5lovelanguages.com[7] and your quick profile test can be accomplished in less than five minutes. This could prove valuable in enhancing husband and wife communication, understanding and intimacy. What language does your heart speak? More importantly, what love language does your heart hear? Many of us have several closely related languages, whereas others may have a definite clear frontrunner. Mastering this is like an interior decorator shopping for high quality furniture that will be used to accessorize the home as it gets closer to completion.

You can do this as the home is still being built. Learn your spouse's language, and then practice speaking it into their heart until you are fluent. This outpouring will cause an overflow that will spill back over into your heart. Remember, rivers flow; lakes are stagnant. Pour out love in a way that it can be received and remember to not look for a quick return. Good stocks provide a steady, long-term return on investment. Invest some time with your spouse and explore your love languages. Take the time to implement what you learn early on, opposed to the fifteen years into marriage we took. #URwelcome.

CHAPTER 11

Learning How to Resolve Conflict

[MJ & KJ] There is a common phrase often used when offense occurs and challenging circumstances present themselves in our relationships: "Get over it." Although this is a novel idea, simply "getting over" something means that it is actually still there. The reality is, most people seek to avoid conflict and choose to sweep un-forgiveness, offense, hurts and disappointments (and whatever you may add to this list) underneath an imaginary rug. This is not a great addition to the home we are constructing and now furnishing. Learning to resolve conflict does not allow us to get over it or even get past it; it requires us to go through it. Whatever "it" is, we are capable of overcoming and transforming misery into ministry.

We have identified what we call the *seven deadly sins* of unre-solved conflict. These are alternate routes both husbands and wives are guilty of taking instead of tackling conflict head on. In this chapter we will identify the seven and map out how Christ's direct path to conflict resolution provides a more accurate and effective route to travel. The seven are:

Silence (silent treatment)

Shutting Down

Store Housing (score keeping or adding things up)

Stock Piling (allowing it to rot)

Suppressing (withholding affection)

Self-Serving (hurt people hurt people; no communication; verbal vomit)

Subject Hopping (can't identify the source of the original issue)

Let's examine how these seven can become stumbling blocks on the road to reconciliation.

1. Silence

[KJ] Conflict resolution is probably one of the most difficult lessons I had to learn firsthand, as I did not see this modeled well for me growing up. I saw family fights and lyrical lashings and witnessed verbal and physical abuse. Conflict for my father's side of the family often ended up in a fight—meaning an actual physical brawl—sometimes escalating into the street. On my mom's side of the family, conflict almost always ended in vocalized lashings that, more times than I care to remember, resulted in someone being verbally bruised or lacerated. Their two-edged swords wielded "verbal zingers;" words that struck and stuck, usually below the belt. This form of "speaking in tongues" was extremely unhealthy and unproductive, the long lasting effects of which were hard to shake. In an attempt to not duplicate the same outcome modeled before me in my childhood, I thought it would be best for me to create an alternate plan of conflict resolution moving forward into our marriage.

Truthfully, when Montell and I were first married, we didn't really know how to resolve conflict well, mostly because we didn't really know how to communicate well. Although my husband studied and was a communication major in college and attained knowledge in the area of conflict resolution, awareness and application were very different things. We did not take the direct or godly path to address our issues, yet through some of those "experiences" (or failures), we learned how to best communicate with each other without leaving carnage. When we were first married, I can recall a seemingly small instance we experienced together that would become one of our most valuable life lessons. It was very painful getting to it, yet extremely productive after going through it.

When I would get home from a long day of work, I would begin cooking a meal and preparing for us to sit down and eat it together. *In my mind,* I believed that if I, "the good wife," cooked a meal, then the "good husband" thing for him to do was to: 1. Show up on time, 2. Call if you will be late, 3. Let me know if your plans had changed or 4. Give me a heads up if you were bringing any other guests home. *In my mind*. I thought that's what automatically happened when you got married, yet I never articulated that to him! Somehow, he never telepathically received the memo.

During this early start in our careers and being newly married, the music industry schedule was rigorous. Almost every night he was either recording late, keeping late nights in the studio and not calling, or sometimes not coming home at all. My attempts to become the happy homemaker left me feeling unappreciated, annoyed and disrespected. In my mind, his hurtful actions were intentional. I was sure he was deliberately abusing and dishonoring my efforts to be a good wife, especially after my advances from the work boardroom to the kitchen cutting board. The most direct path I could have taken to address this issue would have been to say, "Honey, if you're going to be late, absent, or bringing guests, would you mind letting me know? I have been preparing dinners to have with you and this will help me better plan for the evening."

I believe his answer most assuredly would've been, "Sure, honey. No problem!" We all know that would've been too easy! Rather than speak my mind, like words from a famous rap song, I allowed my *mind to play tricks on me*.

Instead, night after night I would go to bed angry and I would give my husband the silent treatment. He didn't even know why I was mad and I didn't know how to express myself, so this volatile cycle would begin. I didn't care to relive my explosive childhood experiences, so I went the opposite direction and opted for silence, hoping to evade conflict.

What I didn't know at that time is when we get mad, we need to talk it out, even if it is painful or not what we have been taught. Early on in our marriage it was not at all uncommon for me to go to bed upset. There were many nights we would go to bed angry and remain restless while sleeping in unresolved issues. What I discovered was that I would wake up the following morning even angrier than the previous night. In my mind, I was attempting to allow the issues to resolve themselves. In actuality, I stewed overnight on the issues, allowing my anger to simmer all night into a light boil I would serve him the next day...especially since he missed the meal I prepared for him the night before. Compound interest can be a good thing; compound anger is not. The word of God instructs us in Ephesians 4:26 to "be angry and sin not." Somehow, I missed the memo.

2. Shutting Down

[MJ] Waking up the next day more upset than the night before, my wife would begin to shut down our communication all together. Now, there were two grown adults walking around the house and no one was speaking to each other. Perhaps we were more like two disgruntled children walking around in adult bodies. Regardless, when something is dysfunctional, for many it is the default reaction to "turn off" until the issue is identified and a remedy is available. I am the type of guy where if I'm driving in my car and an orange or red engine light comes on, I immediately seek to find the issue and resolve the problem. My wife, on the other hand, will see the light, ignoring the possibility of failure and instead decide there is time to continue with no damage to the vehicle so long as it is handled eventually. This actually happened one year as we had our entire family in the car headed towards the Atlanta airport for a family vacation.

I noticed something was definitely wrong with the way the car was handling, but she was certain it was just the alignment. After all, we couldn't fix it then, right? It would be a big inconvenience to our family and our plans, and although it was getting progressively worse (even from just the day before when I drove it and there was nothing wrong with it) it should be able to last until we returned home. In all actuality, a portion of metal from underneath the car happened to be rubbing against the right front tire and while on the 285 freeway in Atlanta in the middle lane traveling at 70mph, the tire exploded. There is no question our car should have flipped over or been hit yet at that moment, all lanes were clear. I miraculously drove across three lanes and pulled over to the side of the road. Ignoring the warning signs and denying the level of severity doesn't make the situation any less dangerous.

My wife would go to bed with her anger traveling 70 mph in a 55 mph zone. The broken parts underneath and within were tearing away and literally shredding at our communication. The ride was getting bumpy, yet I was assured everything just needed to be realigned. We are both speeding towards what we believed should be a vacation and a blissful marriage. Not speaking to each other was common in the marriages modeled before us. After all, Kristin's mom had spoken up in her first marriage, and it sadly and unfortunately ended in divorce. My wife chose to keep silent while the warning signals were flashing like disco strobe lights, and I really believed that if there were a problem, she would come to me and address it. She said nothing. Therefore, there must be no problem. So much for my college degree in communication; this ride was not going to end well. Thank God we had insurance.

3. Store Housing

[KJ] In my silence, I began to store house, or add up all the things that my husband had done wrong that day, yesterday and every day for the previous two years. One way to determine if we are store housing in our marriages is if we find ourselves keeping score. Taking mental notes of how many times we were wronged, what they did to us and exactly when it happened and how we may be able to forgive but not forget the wrong are classic symptoms of store housing. It's like gathering ammunition to prepare an arsenal to wage war against yourself and your spouse. Keep in mind, this scenario is still revolving around a simple miscommunication and an unfilled expectation over prepared meals.

I was now taking note of how many times I cooked and he didn't show and how many times I slaved over a hot stove and he did actually come home but had already eaten. At this point, I had not spoken to him—not even once—to alert him to the frustration that was building. I was hunkering down, awaiting the opportunity to let him have it, yet he apparently had no idea what was coming or why (which means he's either deliberately insensitive or unintentionally naïve). Either way, in the words of a great sailor, "That's all I can stands, and I can't stands no more!" –Popeye

4. Stockpiling

[MJ] My wife stored this information and began to take inventory of all things I had done wrong and how ungrateful I actually was. The annoyance level was now at a place where any error I made was just added to the long list of my accumulated wrongs and shortcomings. Some days we functioned well, but it would only take one mishap to reopen the mental Rolodex and add accrued interest to my accounts payable invoice. Days became weeks and weeks became months, and in this case, even several years would pass without us ever addressing the food prep dilemma. I didn't know this issue even existed, yet the hurt was just beneath the surface. There is an incredibly huge problem that comes along with the storage of foul, unattended and even toxic materials; it begins to rot.

Stockpiling is like throwing a bag of garbage down in the basement or into the trunk of your car and never taking it out and expecting it not to stink. It is impossible! If we don't take the trash out of our home or car -- or in this case, our life -- it will be filled with the aroma of rotting garbage. The accumulation of this stockpiled sanitation is residual, non-recyclable, and has a stench that's hard to remove once we've been exposed to it. We have presented a crazy visual to suggest that with no communication in our young marriage we were speeding while recklessly avoiding the warnings of where we were headed -- the dump.

5. Suppressing

[KJ] I was upset. He was frustrated. Soon we were both so mad at each other I couldn't even remember what the original conflict was about. He certainly had no idea (which only added fuel to the fire). Guys are so different than girls. Sensing a little affection might ease the tension in the home, some nights he would try and cuddle up with me in bed...and I would become even angrier. I was so mad I couldn't even possibly think about being affectionate with him, so I would "withhold myself" (which biblically I didn't even have the right to do, 1 Corinthians 6:19-20). Remember that whole "your body is not your own" thing scripture speaks about? As I continued to stack up the reasons, both old and new, why my spouse had made me so mad, I began to construct an anti-intimacy wall between us, which I assure you was not included in the original blueprint.

I stacked instance after instance up against my husband, just waiting for the opportune time to strike and give him a piece of my mind. He wanted a piece of something else, and certainly my mind *was not* what he was thinking. In retrospect, withholding affection by suppressing our intimacy may have contributed to him resorting to pornography and masturbation in efforts to satisfy himself while remaining faithful to our marriage vows. Of course, he would have to own up to his own weaknesses when this all finally came to light. However, I also took ownership of my role in this scenario.

The open door to entertaining fantasies outside of the marriage, distorted visual imagery in print media and via internet, and seemingly harmless flirtation and fixation on R-rated films are just a few of the symptoms that would begin to surface by not addressing the actual problem. Suppressing intimacy possibly contributed to him suppressing honesty. By not addressing the meal issue (his lack of attention to my dinner efforts), a different appetite would begin to present itself in my husband. I suspect I may not be the only wife who has done this. I would like to tell you that I resolved right away, but it is simply untrue. In fact, I stopped cooking altogether for about two years.

Do you know I never told him why I stopped cooking? I remained offended. I decided that the way to not be offended was to eliminate this issue. I actually stopped cooking! How ridiculous is that? All this came to pass because I did not know how to properly resolve conflict.

6. Self-Serving

[MJ] Oblivious to the cause of the tension that simmered into a slow boil, I did notice my wife stopped cooking. Completely. The kitchen went on strike and we literally did not have a home-cooked meal prepared by her for nearly two years. TV dinners, take out, delivery and fast food became the standard. I knew Kristin was a phenomenal cook because she prepared impressive meals for me when we dated and prior to being married. The fact that the food and the intimacy slowed after marriage had me greatly concerned. However, I had never been married before and had no frame of reference to which I could to compare our marriage. There was no mentorship for us to look to for counsel, and honestly, we weren't walking closely enough to Christ to have that resource available to us in a ministry.

I saw my parents' relationship, which was void of intimacy; naturally, I began to think this was normal. I began to gain weight from unhealthy eating and dealt with self-esteem issues from being the recording artist that all the women wanted, yet I felt rejected at home. Keep in mind, the enemy took a simple misunderstanding, a miscommunication, and sent our lives spiraling down a prideful pathway for several years. It all could have been resolved with an act of transparency and humility. Being self-serving focuses more on winning than resolution and is rooted in the timeless adage that "hurt people *hurt* people."

[KJ] I began to lash out at Montell and try to hurt him because I knew how to hurt him. Proverbs 21:19 says it is "Better to live in a desert than with a quarrelsome and nagging wife." I told him how annoyed I was with him because he hadn't taken out the trash, he had left his clothes in piles all over the floor, he hadn't put gas in the car, or he had spent the previous night out with his friends (instead of coming home). I had to pick up the ball where he dropped it, I had to be both mom and dad for our daughter and to top it all off, I couldn't believe he had left the house without making coffee for the third morning in a row. I would verbally vomit all over him and wonder why our house had become a place of tension and frustration, a place where he didn't want to be. I began to take every little thing personally and then go back into a selfish mindset. I thought, "If he can't meet my needs, why did we even get married?" I couldn't believe our marriage had come to such a desperate place but in actuality, what I had done was turn a molehill into a mountain. As I was serving myself in attempts to preserve my pride, he was seeking external attention and serving himself through unhealthy stimulations, all the while growing more intimate with fame in place of me.

7. Subject Hopping

[MJ & KJ] Years later, the combined tensions in all these areas finally began to boil and spill over from our personal life into our public life. We were great together in business, yet behind closed doors, our marriage was nothing to be admired. Our bedroom paled in comparison to our boardroom skills. When we did attempt to go back and find the original source of contention and strife, we were now faced with a barrage of accumulated symptoms that masked the real sickness. We couldn't even identify where the initial conflict began.

It's hard to hit a moving target. Unable to focus on the genesis of our issue, we resorted to subject hopping, where we both recounted all the things on which we felt the other had missed the mark. This is where we both were prideful and resorted to rehashing our past failures instead of seeking resolution for the present and future. She said "Remember when we were dating and you weren't thoughtful and didn't remember our anniversary?"

He said, "Remember how you used to be before we said *I do*?" In retrospect, all of this was about a husband being late for a dinner a wife had prepared. He didn't show up, so the enemy did. We would have to review a laundry list of disappointments and irrelevant scenarios before arriving to a place where we would choose resolution over being right. Days, months and even years later, we reached serious crisis because we didn't deal with the conflict when it first began.

Although this scenario may seem minor, childish or even trivial, the reality is that this happens in homes all over the country and all over the world where miscommunication and non-communication escalates beyond repair, and we are then left wondering why our marriages are in crisis. This was just one little instance that we had blown way out of proportion and escalated almost beyond repair because of how we handled it. Statistics show that we are not alone in fending off the seven deadly sins of unresolved conflict. This is why it is essential to learn how to resolve crisis swiftly, concisely and in love.

[KJ] Unresolved conflict with my husband proved to be toxic and very detrimental in how we communicated disappointment, hurt feelings and unmet expectations to each other. It's tough to meet expectations when they aren't clearly identified. Our spouses are not mind readers.

I am certain in our story you can find at least one or more identifiable instances that you may apply to how you have behaved with your spouse. These non-communicative practices undermine your everyday walk together and often create rifts that are detrimental, especially in the beginning of your journey together. If you have or are currently involved in this type of communication, it is advisable to stop and reassess how you are communicating with your spouse. Even if uncomfortable, take time to have a serious conversation about your expectations and make some markers that are attainable for you both. Opening this dialogue could be considered,

"Defining the win." Not knowing what the "win" is makes it virtually impossible for you or your spouse to hit the mark.

Disappointment, rejection and unhealthy communication will erode a marriage quickly, and soon your foundation will be sitting on sand instead of the Rock. A house built on sand is easily eroded and tossed about by any wave or storm that comes our way. Throughout the course of our marriages, we will encounter a series of storms that can be weathered and overcome, as long as our foundation is strong. Healthy communication requires that both spouses speak and listen and seek to understand more than to be understood. This is a cornerstone of the foundation of our marriages; learning how to overcome the internal conflicts within our marriage will determine whether we can overcome the external obstacles that come our way. I can only tell you from experience that if we had not learned to overcome these communication obstacles, our marriage would have ended not too long after it began. In order to resolve a problem, we had to acknowledge there was a problem; that's the first step on the road to communication recovery.

Identifying the actual issue prior to presenting the problem allows our spouse the opportunity to participate in reaching the solution rather than feeling pressured into one out of guilt. I have often used this mantra: STOP-DROP-PRAY. It is simple to say and remember, yet not so easy to do. Seeking God for the solution can save much drama if done before striking back with angry words.

After identifying the conflict, I have learned to activate what I refer to as "the Gate." *The Gate* is the garage door I roll up in my mouth to keep the words that should not come out inside. When they come up into my throat, they bounce off the door and go right back down. (Crazy visual, I know, but I had to create this so I would actually do it each time.) For example, Montell may miss a scheduled family event, such as a practice or game for one of the kids, and he may say that I never informed him of the event. Immediately, I roll up that garage door and remain silent and pray, "God, is this my fault or did he just forget?"

Now, here is the key; *I wait*! I wait for the Lord to confirm if I am incorrect and to check my spirit to see if I had failed to communicate the kids' schedule to him. Sometimes it is me that has forgotten and there is nothing worse than getting upset with him because of something I've done. If I lash out at him unjustly, guess who has two beautifully manicured thumbs and is going to get it later on in their prayer time? (Point to myself) *This girl*. That's why I like to ask the question before I react. Now, in the instance where I have told him, I pray for the Lord to please reveal to him what and when I told him. "Please remind him, because I don't want to fuss." Coming from me, it could be viewed as condemnation; coming from a loving God, it becomes conviction.

Lastly, after identifying the conflict and holding my tongue to hear how to respond, I seek the correct timing. I want to seek resolution and not merely react. The timing of when something is delivered is directly related to how it is received. I have rarely seen resolution or repentance come in a public setting or following open spousal confrontation. I suggest for the safety of your marriage to address more serious matters in private so if it goes left, you are in a place where neither of you has an audience. Be careful not to say anything that would harm, shame or humiliate either of you. Always protect your spouse. Early on in our marriage I made the mistake of bringing up something in front of others and his response was much less sensitive than it would have been if he had not felt like I put him on the spot. This *never* ends well!

[MJ] Being unprepared for a major holiday, not providing a thoughtful gift on a birthday, missing an anniversary or failing to acknowledge a special day are all real life happenings I have personally and unfortunately experienced. Yet, unlike the meal preparation example, my wife communicated to me that she felt insignificant and devalued. More than complaining about what I had done, she shared with me how she was made to feel. This allowed blame to be displaced with accountability; I could argue my intent, but not the way she felt. Our life experience allowed us to identify the seven deadly sins of unresolved conflict, yet here are seven life-giving solutions to help bring about resolve that satisfies:

1. Speak
2. Surpass
3. Share

4. Submit

5. Surface

6. Spouse-Serving

7. Spotlight

One year I didn't prepare anything special for Mother's Day. This was a huge error. Instead of silence, this time Kristin chose to *speak* and allow the truth and source of the issue to be identified. She spoke from her heart and told me how she felt rather than what I had done. Instead of shutting down, she chose to *surpass* her anger with love and a belief that my failed efforts were not intentional. In lieu of store housing and stockpiling, she *shared* her frustrations with me and *submitted* the overall outcome to God. Instead of suppressing, my wife allowed the issue to *surface* so the enemy couldn't get a foothold into our intimacy. As she would transition from being self-serving to *spouse-serving*, the Holy Spirit would shine a *spotlight* on the source that had us prepared to begin subject hopping. This would allow our marriage to grow better and not bitter.

[MJ & KJ] One of the most important things we have learned in regard to resolving conflict is to speak to our spouse as if Jesus were sitting in a chair in the room with us. Sometimes we must place an actual chair there with us in the room as a visual representation that Jesus is there, listening to how we treat and speak to each other. This may seem extreme or unnecessary, yet the truth is that He is actually there! If we visualize Him sitting there, we are much more careful of the words we choose, the tone, manner and way we say something and how the message is perceived.

We were once challenged where one of us in the marriage used finances allocated for an outstanding medical bill to purchase a huge (and one might say gorgeous) large screen television. Of course, this was executed without consulting the other spouse. One of us had the right to be furiously mad. However, how this was handled would set the tone for the day, the week and possibly several of our future interactions. A lot of prayer took place. When we were done entertaining guests with our new and sudden addition to the family, we retired to our bedroom for the evening.

The one of us with the two beautifully manicured thumbs (pointing at herself) literally had to visualize Jesus sitting on the bench under the window in our room. As she visualized Him being present there with us, the angry thoughts quickly became much tamer words delivered much differently than how she felt earlier in the day. She presented more passion with less intensity. She even had to take it a step further to temper her response as he explained his rationale. He went on to say that said electronic item was on a super sale, and the deal just could not be passed up.

Prior to exploding, Kristin heard a little voice say, "Watch how you talk to *us*." Immediately, the three-fold cord came to mind. It is not just our spouse we are speaking with; we have to keep that in mind. We are accountable in how we communicate our disappointments, frustrations and anger, especially when it comes to our spouse. We would discuss what the money had been earmarked for and why the unsanctioned purchase caused frustration, as the misappropriated funds might result in a future financial struggle. After not just listening but actually hearing and responding to sincerely resolve the conflict, we both could see the light at the end of the tunnel. This time it wasn't a train.

Communication is a major issue. How a couple communicates can determine the tone of their home, the temperament of their children and the overall happiness of their marriage. Mastering this skill, the art of communicating for conflict resolution, is an absolute game changer. It is important to understand our spouse like nobody else can. After all, this is the person with whom we get to spend the rest of our life.

Do you function in any of the seven? Has unresolved conflict planted seeds of un-forgiveness in your marriage? Are you currently living with offense in your heart towards your spouse? Discuss intimately with God first and invite the Holy Spirit to reveal hidden areas to you that may be harboring fugitive offenses. Then, find the appropriate time to lovingly share with your spouse how what was done made you feel. Address your feelings, not their actions. Let the spirit of God oust the spirit of offense. Finally, begin to utilize the seven solutions to combat the sins of unresolved conflict and watch as others in your marital neighborhood begin to admire how great the house you are building looks on the outside, as it is a reflection of the house cleaning occurring inside. Live so that others desire to use your blueprint plans to design their homes as well.

CHAPTER 12

How to Overcome Offense

Proverbs 18:19 (NLT) - An offended friend is harder to win back than a fortified city. Arguments separate friends like a gate locked with bars.

[KJ] I have never had much of a green thumb, yet my curiosity was peaked for botany many years ago when I first moved to Georgia and saw these beautiful plants as I drove along the freeway. I was informed they were called kudzu. It's actually quite a fascinating plant, as it is a vine that crawls up trees, walls and other plants. It will then wind and intertwine itself all over the host and shade it with its colorful displays. I used to marvel at the beauty of this vine, yet I didn't understand why most Georgians had such disdain for them. It didn't take long for me to realize that these flowers were not as lovely as they appeared. Just as a so –called health food can have more calories than an unhealthy choice, or even how in scripture the enemy can appear as an angel of light, things are not always as they seem. Something that I have marveled at for its beauty was actually a silent killer.

I was unaware that many actually refer to it as "the vine that ate the south." An interesting bit of trivia about kudzu is that the reason it is everywhere is because *you can't kill it.* Spraying and mowing only makes it angry and when you cut it down, it grows back greater and faster. This lush green vine is invasive and once it begins to take over an area, it is literally uncontrollable. The only way to kill it is if you pull it out from the root in the very beginning.

When I think about offense and the damage that it does to a marriage, family or soul, it is like a spiritual kudzu. It grows like an uncontained wildfire and destroys everything in its path, sucking the life from all the things around it, eventually killing it. By keeping its host in shade, or darkness, offense conceals the light and brings death. It allows something unnatural to happen in a natural setting. To keep this from happening in our marriages, we must identify it as it begins so it doesn't get out of control. Similar to kudzu, we must eliminate offense as soon as it appears, pulling it up from its root in order to keep it from spreading to every area of our marriage and ultimately destroying it.

[MJ] Who are the people who tend to offend us the most? Often they are the family and loved ones who are closest to us. Our spouse is probably the most accessible and vulnerable relationship to perpetrate offense against because next to God, he or she is (and should be) the closest person to us. When a person doesn't know us, it's harder for them to deeply offend us. The closer the person is to us, the deeper the wound of offense can be. There is an incredible read by author John Bevere called *The Bait of Satan* that lays a foundation of how the spirit of offense is the primary tool the enemy uses to bring division and destruction to steal from us, kill us and destroy any legacy we could possibly leave. I highly recommend this resource to all who have difficulty forgiving, even to the point of suggesting you stop reading this book to be freed from the bondage of offense and then return to continue building a healthy blueprint afterward. It can be the difference between building this home on sand or upon stone.

This chapter is really that serious. Offense is often the weapon of choice to administer chaos amongst families, relationships and especially within marriages. One reason offense is so dangerous is because it doesn't just happen overnight. Offenses are like little seeds that corrode the foundation at its core. It takes time to germinate, but like the kudzu or a virus, it quickly reproduces and yields some horrible fruit such as bitterness, unforgiveness, anger, rage and revenge (just to name a few). This is not just a pivotal key Kristin and I desire for you to take away from this reading; it is the key to the front door of the godly home our blueprint strives to build. *We need you to get this.*

[KJ] I've seen firsthand what can result from unattended offense. I share my testimony that both my parents had been married six times and divorced five times by the time I was 19. I believe that most of these relationships ended due to seeds of offense that rooted and resulted in producing the fruit of divorce. As we were writing this book, it occurred to me that I had never really thought about how serious this issue was until considering some fundamental facts about my parents' marriage.

Offense surrounded them. Offense between races and cultures consumed our nation during the time my parents were an item. My parents are different races and married at a time when it was not acceptable to marry outside of your race. Paul McCartney and the late Michael Jackson hadn't created the song *Ebony and Ivory* yet and interracial marriage was not embraced. In fact, in many southern states one could be imprisoned for as much as five years for participating in the mixing of races, and black men could be placed in jail for looking at a white woman in the face. Being an interracial couple wasn't popular among their friends, relatives or society at that time. What seems common and acceptable to us now, during the 60's and 70's caused pressure and stresses and even threats of violence that are beyond comprehension.

My parents were ostracized, fired, evicted, mocked, ridiculed and cast out because of being an interracial couple. Now, if you consider the pressure of adding a biracial child into this equation, the seeds of offense were everywhere. It's hard enough in a marriage to overcome the offenses of each other, let alone the offenses of everything and everyone around you. The enemy was working overtime, and he had plenty with which to work. It's unfortunate that offense occurs from external factors, but it's a travesty when it happens internally.

Let's look at the definition of offend:

Of·fend

To cause displeasure, anger, resentment, or wounded feelings in; to cause resentment, humiliation, or hurt; to cause insult, engage in gross insensitivity, insolence, or contemptuous rudeness; to insult openly and usually intentionally.

Offense. It can start with mere displeasure of how you have or perceive you have been treated, words that have been spoken or perhaps even words that weren't spoken. Offense often begins with some sort of violation where we feel we've been wronged and it has not been rectified. If it is not dealt with immediately, innately we feel like there should be some kind of justice for the way that we've been treated. While waiting for justice, bitterness sits in the corner, waiting to pounce on us; this presents the fertile soil for the seed of offense to take root. Sometimes this comes when we hold it in, gossip about it or merely pretend like it didn't happen. Sometimes this can lead to us trying to isolate ourselves from the person who has hurt us as a self-defense mechanism.

When we are isolated, we don't communicate and we may try to avoid the person who offended us, especially when that person is our spouse. This makes for a very hostile environment. Then we try to get other people to see why we feel the way we feel (misery loves company), and we begin to solicit others to gang up on our spouse to confirm the condemnation that is worthy for their behavior. Now we've become the Johnny Appleseed as we have shared the seed of offense and, just like kudzu, it spreads! Over time, an unresolved offense grows into resentment, which can cause us to do unimaginable things (especially to the ones we love the most). I can hear many of you now saying, "No, not me! I could never let it get that far. It's not that serious." I wonder how many people have thought that same thing as they sat across from their spouses and their divorce lawyer or worse yet, in a jail cell after doing the unthinkable. I wonder if these were the thoughts going through Judas Iscariot's head after realizing how he betrayed Jesus. No one ever intends for something to end poorly, yet we know that the statistics rise every day telling us that this issue of offense is a big deal.

Here are just a few of the things we've heard listed as reasons offense occurred:

He or she doesn't respect me.
He or she doesn't tell me they love me.
He told me I'm fat.
He called me by his old girlfriend's name.
He or she always makes fun of me.
She doesn't respect me.
He doesn't make the bed or help me around the house.

She is rude to me.

He or she talks down to me.

He or she says I've changed.

He or she says I can't change.

Have you ever said or experienced having any of these things said to you? These things may seem silly at first glance, yet this is an extremely small list that goes on and on. I've heard these words as couples pour out their hearts over and over again. Something that started as a few simple words and seemingly harmless actions eventually become the preverbal end of the world, especially when administered by someone who means the world. If a small mustard seed portion of faith can move mountains, we can only imagine that the same portion of offense can build mountains. Don't misunderstand me; sometimes there are legitimate complaints. However, there are times when the little things are just blown out of proportion. There are two primary reasons people are offended. We have either been treated unfairly or we believe we have been treated unfairly.

[MJ & KJ] Here are a few suggestions to consider when seeking a remedy for an offensive situation.

Seek to understand rather than be understood. It is always possible that the lens we are viewing an issue from is skewed. Perception is always based on the recipient's understanding of what the deliverer may or may not have intended to convey. It's almost like entering a hall of mirrors and looking into a large warped piece of glass at a carnival. We see a reflection that in no way reflects the actual image. What is being viewed actually becomes distorted. In another example, if one were to stand on a scale fully clothed in winter gear while carrying two bricks and a baby, the numbers that appear on the display would undoubtedly be inaccurate. For an accurate reading, one would need to present himself without the additional baggage and weights that distort the truth.

Try not to dictate intent. How many times have we been guilty of internally drawing a conclusion without having all the information? Have the thoughts, "You did that on purpose," "You meant to do that," or something similar ever crossed our minds? When we engage in this behavior, we are not seeking resolve, but revenge. Internalizing these scenarios will cause us to develop negative thoughts, attitudes and even unhealthy behaviors toward someone (like our spouse) once this seed is planted. In due season, what is planted will bear fruit. This can produce a harvest of bitterness, leading to a season of reaping what was not intentionally sown.

Get over yourself! This one sounds a bit harsh, yet it can be prideful to conclude that we are always the punch line of someone's joke, object of ridicule and the target of our spouse's ill intent. Perhaps some of us have never heard this before, and since we are not married to any of you, we will take the liberty to submit this theory for your consideration: *Sometimes, it's just not about you.*

Grow up! Stop being offended and stop offending! Most times when we are offended, our spouse may be completely unaware of what they've done to offend us. When it's brought to our spouse's attention, more times than not, a godly response is the result. When offense ferments within us, we grow bitter rather than better.

Here is a bold statement: Overcoming offense is the secret to lifelong marriage. Learning to apply this principle means we will be offended. In an earlier chapter, we shared some of our testimony where we experienced heavy trials only to hear God ultimately reveal to us that the test wasn't for us, but for someone else. This is another instance where this may apply to us all. Sometimes, it's just not about us.

We have used the words, "Toughen up, buttercup!" with our son in instances where thicker skin needed to be developed for him to remain competitive in his athletic endeavors. Taking some tough shots from an opponent and being able to shake it off and stay in the game is a learned behavior. The sports world has often instructed that "the best offense is a good defense" and we believe there is a great truth to this. Perhaps knowing offense will come, both intentional and unintentional, will allow us to look beyond the offense and see the person's heart. Remember, hurt people *hurt people*. When we are offended, we can become an offender or become a minister of reconciliation. Although we understand it's not easy, dealing with intentional offenses can be an intentional process of showing love and mercy.

Most people prefer to avoid confrontation. Unfortunately, avoiding the issue won't make the situation any less offensive. There is fine print in the blueprint: Husbands and wives, if something is bothering you in the slightest, we implore you to prayerfully seek immediate resolution. Sometimes we have to put ourselves aside and take a genuine look at what something really is, as opposed to what we have made it to be.

When you are offended, confront the offense. The Bible says if we have an issue with our brother (or spouse) that we are to take it to them. The mistake many of us make in attempting to seek resolution in a hurtful situation is we confront the person instead of the offense. We will say things like, "You did this to me," instead of addressing how the offense made us feel. Once we address the actual issue, if they are unresponsive we are instructed in Matthew 18 to take a witness (someone else) to address it again, as to have another impartial party available to help navigate towards resolution. If the issue remains unresolved, the Bible tells you to seek counsel from a ministry leader or counselor not concerned with choosing sides. It is important to bring in someone who is unbiased and will hear only the facts of the situation without showing favor to one particular spouse.

Keep your flesh in check. When we feel like reacting or overreacting, we need to stop, think and keep our thoughts in check. This means that although we may spiritually desire a positive outcome following the offense, we may humanly, subliminally, desire to hurt those who hurt us. Jesus gives us an example of not seeking to harm those who would do harm to Him, even with bad intentions. Scripture tells us that His ways are above our ways and His thoughts are not our thoughts (Isaiah 55:8). We have to suppress the temptation to get revenge or payback. It is important that we control our thoughts and urges to retaliate in any way. We do understand this is difficult, yet we encourage you to *resist*! Let's make up our minds that when we are offended, we will confront the issue in love and allow ourselves to be confronted in love. As our pastor Dennis Rouse says, "You need to control your stinkin' thinkin' or it will control you."

Be quick to repent and forgive offenses. We should all strive to be quick to listen and slow to speak, just as the brother of Jesus instructs us in James 1:19. Most of us have this backward and are slow to listen and quick to respond. When our spouse tells us they are offended by something we have done, the enemy tries to make us feel offended. Don't take the bait. Let's not be defensive; listen to what they are saying. We may have unintentionally said or done something that could have truly damaged our loved one, and all it would take is a sincere repentance from the action (meaning to turn away from it) to get right with our spouse and back to the regularly scheduled program.

Forgive much, as God has forgiven us. We are not naïve to think that our spouse will never knowingly and intentionally harm us with words or actions. In these instances, what is the appropriate response? What happens if this offense becomes habitual? How can we forgive them? If it seems impossible to you, you are absolutely correct. In our own power, as mere humans, we cannot unconditionally love someone and forgive and forget the offenses done to us, at least not the big stuff. If we could, there would have been no reason for the cross. However, there *was* a reason for the cross. Perhaps some are reading this more for the marital counsel than for spiritual growth. However, we would submit that marital growth without spiritual growth is unhealthy. We encounter many who desire to have God's blessing on their marriage; however, they prefer to disregard the knowledge that comes along with attaining the blessing. They want the growth without the process.

Not all growth is good. Cancer is a growth, but you won't see most people seeking to attain it. The wisest and most well known doctors and psychologists in the world could only attempt to give a natural explanation for the supernatural work God completed in our marriage. That's truth. Outside of Christ, it's impossible to understand this forgiveness phenomenon. Inside Him we are graced to understand that we were born offenders to Christ, and He forgave us and continues to leave an open tab to pick up the past, present and future offenses we commit against God our Father, without a credit limit. This line of credit only remains available to us when we extend that same line of credit to others, especially our spouses.

Perhaps you have been committing the offenses in the marriage. One of the greatest offenses we can commit is to believe that marriage is about our wants, desires and needs. The minute we said "I do," we vowed to be more concerned about someone else and to prefer someone else's feeling over our own and in essence said, "I agree it's not about me." When we think it *is* all about us, we fall into *pride*, which is like *the quicksand of offense*. Pride is the muck we get caught up in that eventually drags and chokes the life out of us in our marriage. It will keep us from admitting that we have a problem or that we may have offended our spouse. Pride can harden our hearts and distort our understanding of what's real. Pride can cause us to believe that we are the victim and that we've been wronged. Soon, we will be justifying our behavior based on how we feel. Even if we have been mistreated, we don't have license to hold on to offense. We can't hold on to offense and Christ at the same time.

[KJ] I can remember my husband asking me to help him with something in his ministry job. We agreed on a set fee that I would be paid as a contractor for my services producing this event. He described what he wanted me to do, but most of the details were pretty vague (sounds like ministry). When I got into the project, I soon realized that the time that I had allotted in my mind to complete this project was not realistic. I ended up spending about 80 hours on the project, as opposed to the 20 I had originally estimated. The event was very successful, and I gave it my all. In fact,

I ended up doing about three jobs instead of one. I'm an all or nothing girl, so I went all in, despite the task requiring more of me than I anticipated.

A few days after the event, I received my check for my participation in making sure the project was done with the spirit of excellence. But a funny thing happened once the payment arrived; I felt slighted. Why did I feel that way? I knew exactly what to expect. As I stepped back and looked at it, I realized that I felt that way for a number of reasons:

What was being asked of me was not clearly defined. I ended up doing three jobs instead of one, which is what the initial fee quote was based on. I had given it my best, and because of that, I felt I deserved more. The problem was that I didn't share my expectation or frustration with him. I went the extra mile on my own accord -- not because he asked me. So how in the world could I expect him to read my mind?

The truth is, I couldn't. The root of this offense was based on my own thoughts, my own decisions and my lack of communication about the way that I felt. Truthfully, many offenses start with the root of entitlement. If I'm completely transparent (and that was a little hard to swallow), that was 100% true about me in this instance. I felt the church didn't value what I had brought to the table. Didn't they know what I did in the music business prior to ministry? Had they not seen my résumé? Were they deliberately devaluing my gift to the ministry and did they not understand this payment for my services rendered would be considered insulting in my previous profession? Surely my husband realized what he was asking me to do should have garnered at least a "Thank you" or "Atta girl" from the executives. My mind continued to kudzu.

Instead of dealing with the offense immediately, I added insult to injury and waited about a month or so. More events happened within that timeframe; it's safe to say that the offense that I harbored led to a little less than lackluster performance on the next two events. After reaching a peak of frustration, I begin to share my offense with my husband. I soon realized it wasn't him or the ministry that was the problem; it was *me*. Past ministry hurts from a previous church, unacknowledged services rendered and going from an ordained minister in that prior church to now being unrecognized in my current church all contributed to my offense in the place where I wanted to be serving with joy. It's what I did when I first arrived there and had a heart to do without compensation. What changed?

The spirit of offense remained dormant and seemingly came from nowhere and was now attempting to take the breath from a ministry that allowed me to breathe again. I had to repent. I repented to God and to my husband. I had to own the way I had felt, the way I behaved and apologize for what I had done. But what if I had never said anything? How long would this have carried on? What else would it have cost me? The enemy is cunning. What initiated as something small could have become even bigger than it did.

How many times do we all allow little things to become big things? We must ask ourselves if it's really worth it.

[MJ & KJ] When we choose to live an offended life and not get it right with our spouse, we are also not getting it right with God, our other covenant partner. This often indicates one of two things: 1) We are choosing to remain offended over forgiving and 2) We are rejecting the forgiveness Christ offers to us. Mature believers cannot actively be in the word and not take action against offense. Throughout scripture, we are reminded that offenses will come. It doesn't say it might come or may come, but that they will come. It's a guarantee. It also says *"woe to those who plan iniquity," (Micah 2:1, NIV).* Both sender and receiver of offense get to play a part in something that is certain to come, especially in our marriages. These trespasses will probably even cause us to go beyond the 7 times 70 forgiveness rule, yet to be more like Christ and build our marital foundations on stone and not sand, we should keep the forgiveness of offense tab open so that the one offered to us also remains limitless.

Historically, the word shows us examples of how those who could have remained offended instead chose to change the course of history. Joseph could have chosen to be offended by his brothers' betrayal instead of seeing it as part of God's plan for his life and eventually saving his entire family. Job could have chosen to be offended and stop praying for his friends after their accusations that his plight was caused by some hidden sin he had committed against God. The Bible shares many accounts that would have never been recorded had the chosen leaders not overcome their offense.

What offense have you not overcome? What great story and testimony are you potentially abandoning while refusing to overcome offense by forgiving? What life-giving example are you aborting by refusing to forgive? When we choose to remain offended, we forfeit our story that someone else will surely rewrite.

There is no offense too great to work out. It is not easy to overcome offense, but it is surely necessary. Offense will come; how will we handle it? Our choices and actions will determine how stable one of the core building blocks of your marriage will be: forgiveness. Love covers a multitude of sins, including offense. We must be careful not to offend our spouse but if we do, we should be quick to repent and ask for forgiveness. When we operate in love and grace we will get to experience the freedom that Christ has intended for our marriage. This will result in joy, peace, love and much more.

Are you carrying offense? Take some time to review if something may be presently

on your mind, just beneath the surface or buried deep within that may be hindering your marital growth due to offense. It may be a perceived offense, or justified. Regardless, the freedom in forgiveness is available to us all. There is more we will discuss later regarding forgiveness, so take the time to review if your life is holding on to something done to you or something you have done to your spouse that is offensive and needs to be released. It may even be something of which you are unaware. Ask Holy Spirit to reveal it to you. Once you are aware of the offense, you may better prepare for extraction. Use the blueprint tools provided in this chapter and begin releasing yourself and your spouse from the bondage of offense.

CHAPTER 13

Marriage Myths

"The only things perfect about marriages are the air-brushed wedding photos!" -Anonymous

Myth:

An idea or story that is believed by many people but that is not true; A traditional story, especially one concerning the early history of a people or explaining some natural or social phenomenon and typically involving supernatural beings or events.

[MJ & KJ] Perhaps for her, it was prince charming riding in on his trusty stallion and sweeping her off her feet. Possibly for him, a supermodel from the cover of the ESPN swimsuit edition fell madly and passionately in love with him. They both might have envisioned the lovely house on the hill, surrounded by a white picket fence with

2.5 kids and a dog, and possibly even imagined fireworks igniting with each and every kiss. Sounds idyllic, right?

Unfortunately, what we believe marriage could and should look like does not always resemble the truth. We all may have these well-thought-out dialogues as to how our marital conversations should go and disagreements be resolved, along with the script of what we believe should be said and done in our marriages. Although we all may have landed the role of a lifetime, this is no act; yet somehow, the curtain is up and everyone is watching.

The reality is that between "I do" and "they both lived happily ever after" rests something called a *lifetime*. This *lifetime* is rarely considered when couples are entering into marriage vows. The option of divorce is so common that it causes the *lifetime* to now have an expiration date prior to the shelf life God intentionally designed for it. The sobering idea of a blissful eternity together (less the unmentionable sights, sounds and smells shared between husband and wife) is normally polished nice and shiny and neatly wrapped into a huge red bow and presented to the unsuspecting couple without presenting the accurate truths that they may later use to opt out of their commitment within the covenant.

If we don't like our cell phone service, we breach the contract, pay a termination fee and move on to the next device. Sadly, many men and women view marriage the same way. Most often our upbringing plays a role in the way we view marriage and divorce. Through the media, we also see our music and entertainment heroes portrayed in musical chair scenarios where wives are swapped and exchanged like leased autos, and children are adopted, blended and broken apart like an infancy chop shop. This represents a huge portion of today's modern family, where "I do" actually means, "I do...until I don't."

Sometimes there is no real basis of truth to what we believe other than what we have witnessed and been taught, healthy or unhealthy, about marriage. If we declare that God is at the center of our marriages, then our rotting thoughts can begin to spoil the core of our foundation. We both saw marriage through the lenses and the perspectives that we had seen growing up.

The same way it is difficult to fully appreciate sunshine without experiencing rain, it can be challenging to determine what a healthy marriage looks like without identifying what is unhealthy. We decided to share a few of the marriage myths that we have encountered, heard about and personally experienced that can be a source of misinformation going into and sustaining a Godly marriage. We have said continuously that "*Success* is when we achieve something and *experience* is when we fail at something." We are again prepared to share our *experience* to allow us all to expose some common marriage myths that could be potential land mines in even the strongest of marriages.

Marriage Myth #1: We can choose Mr. or Mrs. Right

[KJ] When we are searching for Mr. or Mrs. Right, it is extremely easy to place unrealistic expectations on someone. Choosing our soul mate over the designer of our soul and the mate He created specifically for us may result in us praying for God to bless something He never created for us to enter into. This is why I suggest subscribing to the "*thy* will be done over *my* will be done" theory every time.

> *Trust in the Lord with all your heart; do not depend on your own understanding. Seek His will in all you do, and He will show you which path to take. Proverbs 3:5-6 (NLT)*

When we rely on what God has for us, it will always be better. This is where the sovereignty of God comes into play. He knows what we don't know, and therefore, we may trust Him. Proverbs leads me to believe that there are many pathways that we may choose and without seeking His wisdom, we can find ourselves outside of His will for our lives. For example, I personally preferred to let God choose the one He had for me opposed to me choosing who I had for me.

You see, when I first met Montell, he wasn't what I had in mind. Thankfully, God knew better than me. The story of *How Montell met Kristin* always garners laughs, as we were an unlikely pair upon our first meeting. I have, however, finally admitted that I experienced love at first sight... on our second date. What I understand now is when God chooses for us, we'll never have to ask ourselves or wonder if we are with the right person. God takes out all the guesswork. This allows us to use all our efforts and energies bettering, enhancing and enjoying making our marriage masterpieces without placing a question mark behind our spouse's name. To be superbly honest, there is no such thing as a perfect mate or Mr. or Mrs. Right. If there were, they would cease to be perfect the moment they hooked up with us!

We often make choices based on what's right for us right now. This is not wise, as we don't know what's to come so we don't know what we're going to need. Consider allowing the One who knows what's to come to choose the appropriate spouse for what's coming. Taking this decision out of God's hands and placing it into our own may lead to a common tragic story where we find that Mr. or Mrs. Right is actually only Mr. or Mrs. *Right Now.*

Marriage Myth #2: People automatically grow closer with time

[MJ] Thinking that people automatically grow closer with time is no more accurate than thinking if you sit on the couch watching fitness programs day after day and year after year that you will somehow get muscles. That sounds ludicrous, doesn't it? Chances are we will just take on more of the characteristics of the comfortable couch! For some odd reason, many believe that time will make us automatically grow closer in marriage. As humans, we are all individuals who possess unique desires and needs. Marriage unites these individuals and seeks to find a harmony in combining these unique desires and needs into an agreeable set of attainable goals for our covenant relationship.

A sad truth is that sometimes, time causes people to grow more apart than together. This usually happens when individualism is embraced over the marital union. "What about *my* happiness? What about what's good for *me*?" Any substantial relationship, especially a marriage, takes time, effort and energy to move from *me and my* to *we and us*. This may be achieved through sacrifice, submission, and servant hood. This means taking the *time* to sacrifice our personal needs and desires to prefer the needs and desires of our spouse. We must make the *effort* to submit and defer to our spouse's desires and needs over our own. Finally, we must apply the *energy* to serve our spouse rather than seeking to be served.

[KJ] An untested marriage will have very little testimony. Marriages grow strong by overcoming trials and tribulations, over-communicating so that you can better navigate through life's challenges together on one accord, and continually overlooking our spouse's imperfections as we continue to define our likes and dislikes. If we want our marriages to work, we must work at it with everything we have. It's during the testing and trials where the close bonds are created. I can tell you some of the most trying times were when we became the closest.

For example, when we lost our son Canaan four months into the pregnancy, it was one of the most difficult times of our lives. In fact, I think we both cried for two straight weeks or more. In that trial and tribulation, we learned to lean on one another, to rely on God and to trust we would somehow become stronger once we reached the other side. These circumstances are not meant to break us but to make us; often we can't understand the magnitude of the storms until we weather them and actually get through them. It is only then we realize that we are durable and more resilient because of the endurance required to navigate tragedy. If we will allow it, life's unexpected valleys can create an even stronger bond when traveled together.

Marriage Myth #3: I can change them

[MJ] True heart transformation happens from the inside out. The late Maya Angelou once said that "when someone shows you who they are, believe them." Yet time and time again we choose to ignore personality flaws and character traits that we don't agree with because we believe that they will change after marriage. We often are willing to give someone the benefit of the doubt when, in reality, *there is no benefit in doubt*. Humans can desire change in someone, yet only God creates lasting change. We can adjust, alter and modify our behaviors to appease our spouse, yet true transformation only comes from within and is initiated from within Him.

My wife has spoken about my habit of forming piles in the corner of the bedroom. I can't explain how they happen; they just do. Rather than utilizing the dirty clothes hamper, if I deem an article of clothing worthy of revisiting, I will allow it to stay in the corner. After traveling on business, I will return home and the garments I journeyed with will remain in the corner of the room, right next to the clothing of which I just spoke. Perhaps a pair of shoes won't quite make it to the closet either. Even as I write these words, I am looking over at an accumulation of clothing that has covered nearly 1/3 of wall space from the floor up. I am not proud of this, and I am well aware it is a behavior that my wife greatly dislikes and has for the past 20 years. I have made efforts to alter this behavior. She has made efforts to alter this behavior. I can do well for a time, yet I always find myself reverting back to this behavior. I am guilty of subscribing to external change without fully embracing authentic transformation. She would change this behavior immediately if she could, but this change can't come from me or from my wife.

My wife misplaces things. I am a creature of habit; Kristin is not. Her keys, cell phone, jewelry, that thing she was just holding 10 seconds ago (the baby) and most things are set in random places and not easily found. This drives me nuts. I even experimented and we now have a key bowl in our home that everyone must place their keys in upon entering the house. This is effective, yet not long-lasting. This is because it has prompted an outward response to an internal behavior. I don't know why this action exists in her any more than why I make piles. If I could change it, I would. Once again, this can't come from my wife or me.

This last example goes back to when Kristin and I were dating. I thought she dressed sexy. Once we got married, she would put on an outfit that was flattering, yet in my insecurity, I felt she didn't have to dress like that anymore. We got into a huge disagreement because I wanted to *control her* by imposing my opinion and my will upon her by attempting to use our marriage to cover my insecurity.

It's pretty easy to identify the things we don't like and would like to change in our spouse. What piles do you have in your life? What habits and behaviors are you aware of that could be button-pushing actions toward your spouse? Perhaps there are blind spots that we are unaware of as well. True transformation occurs in the heart. What is in the heart then becomes what we think. What a man thinks, he becomes. This is why we ask the Lord to come into our heart, and not our mind; our mind must be renewed daily. If we think we can change someone, chances are we believe to some measure that we are that person's god. We can be catalysts for change, yet ultimately, that change only occurs when it is activated by our Father.

Is our spouse overly flirtatious with individuals outside of the marriage? Does our spouse drink a bit too much socially? Can they become embarrassing in public? Are they occasionally verbally or physically abusive in private (or in public)? If these things are potential flags prior to marriage, loving the person is not a green light to enter into covenant with them thinking we can change them. This is an opportunity for God to transform prior to saying, "I do." If we are in a marriage where these unhealthy behaviors exist (along with countless others), this once again is opportunity to see the healing and transformational power that is greater than our prompting, nagging and temporary glimpses of success where we get the desired result. We can change ways, but God changes hearts.

Marriage Myth #4: Marriage roles are based on gender

[MJ & KJ] This is one of the greatest misconceptions within marriage! Strong marriages are a collaborative effort. Determining what each husband's and wife's roles and responsibilities will be is important to consider before ever even getting married. At the very least, a plan should be discussed. We should be flexible in the roles that each spouse will play in our marriage, and also under-stand that as we change with life, these roles change as well. Each person needs to be dedicated to the improvement of themselves as individuals as well as the collective unit. Each person has indi-vidual strengths and weaknesses. Letting each spouse use his or her strengths is a great way to delegate responsibility.

For example, if the wife is greater in finances, why should the husband handle the money if that is not his strong suit? Sometimes gender roles are modeled for us in our youth, and we grow to believe that's just how things are supposed to be. The man works, and the woman stays home and takes care of cleaning the house and raising the children. You had better believe Wilma had better have the brontosaurus burgers hot and ready after Fred worked a long hard day down at the rock quarry. We are saying that many modern families have homes where both spouses may have careers, and determining what the care of the home will look like may not be the traditional "Flintstone-prehistoric model" to which many still subscribe. Attempting to implement measures that will not work for your household could be a recipe for disaster.

[MJ] I enjoy ironing. I can't explain why, but I am at peace when starching, steaming and creasing wardrobe for any occasion, including socks and underwear. My wife will often ask me to iron something for her, and although it may appear to be an act of service to her, it is simply natural for me. Perhaps this is the same domestic impulse that also drives me to cook and to vacuum the rugs in our home as well. Where many may consider these traits to be more feminine, *this arrangement works for us.* In contrast to this, when our car is low on fuel my wife will go to the gas station and fill 'er up! She may also be found shooting baskets with our son Skyler out in the backyard or with a hammer and nails attempting to fix something that could be considered more male gender specific. Once again, *this arrangement works for us.* We must all assess our marriage responsibilities on a case-by-case basis and set up rules and boundaries that we can live by. It's easier to stay in your lane when you know where your lane is.

[KJ] In addition, if one spouse's contribution within the home is out of proportion to the other spouse, it can cause an imbalance. For example, take a wife who works, takes care of the children, cleans the house, grocery shops, cooks and runs errands while the husband's role is simply to work and that's it. It won't take long before this marriage feels unbalanced. Lack of definition to each other's roles in a marriage can erode the foundation of a marriage very quickly. Usually when we see this kind of imbalance and predisposition to unfairness, it is perpetuated from something mimicked or learned from our childhood. Let's define our roles and make sure they're balanced where we both can live without being or becoming bitter. I tell my kids all the time, "Be better, not bitter!" Learn not to major on the minor. Marriage is a series of give and take, and there must be sacrifices and compromises in order to meet common ground. Establishing clear goals early on makes it easier to hit the mark and be successful in our marriages!

Marriage Myth #5: Marriage cures loneliness

[KJ] For me, this was one of the lies I believed wholeheartedly. Truthfully, it's one of the areas where I still have to battle to keep my thoughts under control. Growing up in a single-parent home allowed me to see loneliness up close and personal, more often than I'd like to admit. Reacting to this, I vowed early on in life that I never wanted to be lonely. This declaration would haunt me for most of the beginning of my marriage, as I believed my husband would fulfill every void space in my heart.

Here's a newsflash: *God didn't design our spouses to complete us.* I know that may have been a revelation to some of us. Jerry Maguire messed it up for everybody. Our spouse cannot fill every space of loneliness inside of us; *it is God that completes us.* The covenant relationship is between three, not two. If we try and put our spouse in the position to fulfill what God seeks to provide, we are actually creating our spouse to be an idol in place of God and putting him or her in harm's way. That's why God said that He is our comforter. I spent many years trying to fill the space in my heart that could only be occupied by God.

First, I would try and fill it with things. I would try to shop my loneliness away. When Montell was out of town, I would be at the mall. By reviewing our credit card statements, one could see the evidence of me trying to fill idle time and space with material things. His touring credit card charges were room service, and mine were shoes or handbags. The truth of the matter is there's no amount of things that can fill the space that only God was intended to fill.

Once I realized I was trying to fill that hole of loneliness with things, you'd think I would have figured it out, right? Instead of shopping, I just switched my vices, and I began to fill the void *with food*. This was no more effective than my shopping. The more I ate, the emptier I felt. The more weight I gained, the less happy I became. I was trying to fill a God-sized hole with a man-sized solution. I would venture to say that loneliness is a heart condition, not a place that a spouse (or anyone else) can fill. If we don't get it under control, this can be a source of contention because he/she is not designed to meet all our needs. If we can remove this expectation from the beginning, our course will be much easier.

[MJ] My mom is now happily married, and I'm extremely proud of her. She is a living testimony that God can redeem our choices. She gave birth to me four days before her 18th birthday and began as a single mom. I would be the first of four children, and to this day, I have not met my biological father. It would take a divorce after 25 years, and then a remarriage that would end in her second husband's tragic death on the job before she would again find a true love who is now the love of her life. She has been on quite a journey. I can recall one day prior to this state of happiness when she shared something with me that I never really could seem to shake. It was a simple statement that because her mom (my Nana) had spent many years alone, she never desired that for herself. She once said to me, "I'd rather be with the wrong person than to be alone." These words took root in me and began to grow and bear fruit that I never imagined I was capable of harvesting.

When I was touring, I found myself away from home for long periods of time. I suffered from tremendous loneliness. I tried to fill that time with friends, activities, alcohol and eventually, any resource available to pass the time. I even entertained unhealthy relationships—not for the joy of sinning—but to avoid the same thing my mom avoided: being alone. At the time, I didn't recognize this genetic curse as a spiritual battle, and so I attempted to fight it with the power of my flesh. I was willing to be in bad company rather than no company at all. What I failed to realize was that Jesus was seeking to fill the space I stuffed with things that would never satisfy me, things that drew me further from my wife and from Him.

I was not in the word of God during that time in my life. I was saved and confessed with my mouth and believed in my heart that Christ was my savior, yet knowing this and walking in this truth are very different things. I claimed Him with my mouth, yet my heart was far from Him. The distance we feel absent from the Father is often mistaken for human loneliness, so we may attempt to humanly fight what is actually a spiritual battle. Perhaps many are reading this passage who may not subscribe to Christian principles, yet you are experiencing this void of which my wife and I speak. If this sounds familiar, I submit to you that you have nothing to lose and everything to gain by considering what we both found to be the remedy and lifelong solution to our loneliness woes. Consider Christ as a solution.

Marriage Myth #6: Sex & Romance will always be alive in a "good marriage"

[MJ & KJ] I know we would all like to believe this one but, unfortunately, it's just not true. No one feels romantic and sexy all the time. That's only in the movies... and let's face it, even actors can't get it right in real life! It is easy to lose sight of romance when we get bogged down with our day-to-day lives. The hustle and bustle of picking up the kids, running errands, work and the to-do list can all be culprits of stealing the romance. We are not saying we shouldn't strive for it each day, but really, no one feels romantic every single day. There are peaks and valleys in everything, including romance. God designed us to fall in and out of love. We will fall in and out of love with our spouse throughout the duration of our marriage; we believe this is to keep things exciting and fresh. It would suck if we were only able to experience the joy and pleasure of falling in love just one time only. For this reason, God desired and designed for us to experience falling in love over and over again—yes, with the same person.

[KJ] After I had my first child, I by no means felt romantic. The way my body felt, the sleepless nights, breast-feeding, the daily routine and even post-partum depression would all become hindrances to me feeling "in the mood." The challenge was to not allow those feelings to fester for too long as they may consume our thoughts and we become them. Every day we must be intentional to not allow circumstances and situations to hinder our romantic and sensual feelings. We have been married over 20 years. This is difficult no matter how many years one has been married, but it's something that we need to keep in mind at all times. Neglecting this physical, sensory aspect of intimacy may present an open door for our spouse to have wandering eyes or unhealthy fantasies and possibly be a gateway into unhealthy social media interaction with pornography and other means of visual or physical stimuli. The needs of our spouse don't go away just because we don't feel like it. Sometimes we have to make a conscious effort to create an environment or dress up and put on makeup to make ourselves feel pretty and desirable. We may even seek the third-party in our covenant relationship (Holy Spirit) to give us the desire for our spouse when we feel less than ready.

When we feel good inside, it manifests outside. Feeling sexy and beautiful internally reveals itself externally. Men are typically visual (what they see) and women are more typically audio (what they hear). So ladies, it is important to get yourself back together, do your hair and put on something cute that will set the tone for him for romance. Fellas, present yourself well groomed and remember: It is important that she hears how beautiful she is, how much you miss her, how much you value her--and this does not begin in the bedroom! Trust me, she will hear your actions far more than your words. The intentional husband can combine both words and action to prepare his wife for the intimacy and satisfaction both parties may desire and enjoy. Keep in mind that preparation is key! If the intent is to be romantic that evening, consider starting in the morning or perhaps sooner to set the atmosphere. Preparing her mentally creates a physical enjoyment for both spouses. Montell and I are 20 years into our marriage, both over 40, and we cur-rently have a two-year old... so we know this works!

Marriage Myth #7: Marriage means you are happy all the time

[MJ & KJ] It saddens us to see oft times marrieds are the unhap-piest people in the room. Considering that the word tells us, "He who finds a wife finds a good thing and obtains the favor of the Lord," some couples make God's favor appear unfavorable. We believe that this blueprint works if we work it. We also believe that happiness is more than just a feeling; it's a choice. Each day we are given the opportunity to determine our outlook on life, no matter what life itself looks like. We must cause this life to respond to our happiness rather than our happiness being based on our response to life. We were made in the image of our Heavenly Father and He built emotions into us. He delights in us, yet can also be jealous for our affections when we choose the world over Him, be in opposi-tion to us when we are prideful and even show wrath when His people choose sin over salvation. In other words, God is not happy all the time, so we won't be either.

Our spouse cannot be our sole source of happiness. If we are placing our hope for happiness in another person, we may find many days of discouragement. Our spouse can provide many moments of joy, happiness and enjoyment, yet they shouldn't be the source of these feelings. Personal happiness comes from our proximity to God. Marriage can complement happiness, but it cannot be your sole or primary source of happiness. This is very similar to what we talked about earlier in regards to loneliness; no person can fill a hole that only God is designed to fill. The key here is that if a three-fold cord is not easily broken, recognizing God as the third party in our marriage makes the likelihood of experiencing happiness much more realistic.

Marriage Myth #8: Married couples know each other inside and out

[KJ] There is no statement that could be further from the truth. Just because we get married doesn't mean that we can read each other's minds. We have to communicate and tell our spouse what's important to us. He is not a mind reader, nor is she. If we have not told them something, we can assume they do not know. I can share that even after 20 years of marriage, we learn new things about each other every single day. That's part of the adventure! Learning new things about our spouse is refreshing and keeps things fun and interesting.

For example, after 19 years of marriage, I learned that one of my husband's biggest pet peeves is mismatched socks. With a middle school son sneaking into his sock drawer (as well as myself on occasion), it annoys him to no end to have mismatched socks. That seems ridiculous to me, but to him, it is a constant source of contention. For me, I like to have the bed made before we leave the house.

It drives me crazy to come home to an unmade bed. He didn't figure this out until year 15. Why? Because I didn't tell him that it was something that was important to me -- something so simple could have saved me years of aggravation. Exactly how would he know that about me? How would I have known that about him? The only way we will know these things is if we talk about them.

While socks and bed sheets are small topics that can bring about discrepancies, what about the larger issues that go unspoken? We need to discuss things like: How often we will have sex? How will we discipline our kids? Spankings or time out? How and when do we like our meals? All these things may seem trivial, but over time, they matter to the overall happiness of the marriage. The more we know, the better off we are. Be reminded that figuring out our spouse is not the destination, but it's the journey towards learning and knowing each other that brings the most enjoyment.

Marriage Myth #9: Happily married couples don't argue

[MJ] Conflicts and issues will arise in *every* marriage. It's how we respond and resolve these challenges with love, kindness and fairness that will result in whether or not we have a happy marriage. The way we treat each other will determine whether we live in a wounded or a strengthened household. Getting through these things can actually bring us closer together or tear us apart. Conflicts will arise and cause disagreements: deciding to financially help a friend or loved one, budgeting issues in our finances, whether to go on vacation or not, whether to send the kids to private school or public. One thing is for certain: There will be no shortage of conflict.

Differences of opinion can be the source of heated discussion. The way we handle the conflict is what will determine how successful, peaceful and long lasting our marriage can be. This is a relationship that we're in for the long haul. "Till death do us part," remember? Let's not allow disagreements to bring that death sooner than later!

In order for our marriage to last, we must take care of it. Many guys take better care of their cars than their wives; many women take better care of their hair than their husbands. When we truly value something, we take care of it, take time with it, nurture it and make sure it's a priority. Something to keep in mind when conflict arises: always fight fair and remember, nobody gets to leave the mat without resolution. In the marriage fight, reaching a split decision always outweighs crowning a winner and loser.

Marriage Myth #10: Having a baby will fix everything

[KJ] When my husband and I counsel young couples, we often advise them to make sure they spend the first couple of years getting to know each other before considering having a family. Adding a child to a joyful, healthy marriage can add more joy; adding a child to a complicated, unhealthy marriage can add more complications. Using a pregnancy to heal brokenness in a relationship is like placing a Band-Aid over a stab wound. This principle is no different than one I learned long ago about money.

Money does not change a man; it only enhances what was already there. Babies do not change a marriage; it only enhances what is already there. So if there is conflict, turmoil and chaos before the child, this becomes magnified and it only gets more intense when adding a baby. In contrast, if there is love, peace and joy prior to the baby, the atmosphere of love, peace and joy will prevail in the home. This healthy addition can be like drawing a guest wing onto our blueprint, a modification that enhances the structure of the home and raises the value of the property. When adding a baby to an unhealthy structure, the pressure gets turned up even more by the lack of sleep, extra finances, the way our bodies feel, the uncertainties of life and the list goes on and on. Remember the cracks in the dam we talked about in chapter 5? If the marriage is not solid to withstand this new addition, the weight of responsibility and unpreparedness could burst the dam wide open.

[MJ] The reality is that children don't automatically repair a marriage; God repairs marriages. Using a pregnancy to heal something God seeks to heal potentially places that child in the position of becoming an *idol*. There are countless accounts of relationships where a woman is seeking to keep a man committed in the relationship and will allow herself to be impregnated, believing it will cause the man to stay out of obligation rather than love. "Having a baby will fix it" is not wisdom. Please consider having children once you have a loving and understanding relationship established, and then seek to expand and share your love on another level. Children are truly a blessing when they are not a response to fixing something broken. Instead of having a baby to heal the marriage, allow God to heal the marriage and add the baby as a blessing.

Marriage Myth #11: Love will be enough to keep us together

[MJ & KJ] We are reminded of an old Captain & Tennille song titled, "Love will keep us together." Funny (but not funny) -- after 39 years of marriage, the recording duo filed for divorce in January 2014. Apparently, unless that *love* is the love of Christ, even nearly four decades of marriage is prone to failure. We shared that there is a process of falling in and out of love over the course of our marriages in order to experience the pleasure of falling in love time and time again with our spouse. This elaborate blueprint design was constructed for us to feel like we are walking into a brand new home over and over again. Moments when we don't feel "in love" are not signs that our marriage is over. Those moments present opportunity for us to fall in love with our spouse all over again. Sadly, the divorce rate confirms that the resolve to separate is embraced nearly more than it is rejected.

Many couples think marriages should be easy and that we shouldn't have to work at it. Love should be enough; after all, that's what got us into this arrangement. Nothing that is worth it is easy.

We have never heard of an NFL or NBA player making it to the big leagues *because it was easy,* no matter how skilled he may have been. It is no different in marriage. If we don't work at it, it won't work. Usually, if something is easy, it won't last. Marriage consists of two people with differing core belief systems being merged together to create a new value system within the covenant of marriage. This is not going to be easy, but it is going to be worth it if we work hard. We must put in the effort, time and energy to making our marriages a success.

Despite the things we see in movies, on television, through social media and in the unhealthy relationships that surround us, it *is* going to take more than just love to keep us together. Many people don't believe that God is love. When He is the definition of love, then the paradigm shift required to allow this statement to become a truth is indeed possible. Love *can* keep us together. Outside of this definition of love, we are subject to emotional feelings and the cares of life that will cause us to believe that love has come and gone. If the word promises us in Hebrews 13:5 that "He will never leave us or forsake us," how then can love have come and now be gone? If we believe God is love, love will always be enough to keep us together.

We could easily write a book simply solely on marriage myths, so this chapter surely doesn't cover all of the myths couples believe. Just remember, we all come from different places, different backgrounds and are completely different people and now, in our marriages, we are coming together to become one person. This is going to be a challenge, but it's going to be the best challenge of our lives. In order to make our puzzled marriages into a *master-peace*, we have to work at it piece by piece. It is one of the most rewarding relationships we will ever experience and is certainly worth overcoming the myths that could create hindrances to having a successful marriage. We shared these myths with you because these are things that we have personally struggled with and overcome! We hope it will be helpful for you to know some of these falsehoods ahead of time. It is easier to navigate the battlefield if you have some indication of where the land mines are located.

As you read this chapter and you see an area where something resonates in your spirit, thank God for exposing the myth and showing you the hidden trap seeking to do you and your spouse harm. Without hesitation, avoid or diffuse the bomb. We are at war with an enemy that wants our marriages. *Your marriage.* You are not in this fight alone. The word is your instruction manual; this book is merely a map to help you build your marriage foundation and make you aware of possible attacks. We have our marching orders; no marriage left behind! Godly husbands and wives, you are equipped to win this battle... and *that is no myth*!

CHAPTER 14

The Intimacy Factor

in·ti·ma·cy: Close, familiar, usually affectionate, or loving personal relationship.

[MJ & KJ] Intimacy is not limited to human relationships. When hearing the word "intimacy," many immediately think of sexual relationships. Although we will be addressing this topic, we should be aware that we can be intimate with not just people but also things. We can become intimate with anything we spend time with, are familiar with or invest our energy getting close to. Intimacy entails more than just a close physical presence, but requires an exclusive mental and sometimes spiritual connection as well.

Have you ever been in a crowded restaurant with someone before, yet your physical, mental and spiritual awareness of each other made it feel like you were the only ones in the room? We have too! Something as simple as holding hands in a public place can create a private, intimate moment, regardless of the external circumstances. Intimacy requires more than just atmosphere; attention, awareness and being "all in" create some of the closest and most memorable moments we may share with our spouse. Intimacy is the ability to look beyond our loved one's external status, appearance and state of mind and connect on a deeper level. Intimacy. *In-to-me-see*. Intimacy is developed through proximity, access and spending time.

[KJ] Intimacy can occur when achieving close proximity to a person or a thing. Take, for example, my husband and the game of football. He absolutely loves the game of football! He not only enjoys football, the stats, watching it and playing it but he also knows all the players, including the ins and outs of the game. One could say he has an intimate relationship with football. Year after year he grows closer to the game, and therefore, he has developed a deep affection for the sport. In order to be close to my husband, I had to make some decisions to overcome what I am naturally interested in to become closer to him. Despite my deep-seeded love of basketball, you can probably guess what I have now learned to be passionate about. Are you ready for some football!?

One of the things I have learned in these last two decades is that it is important to be passionate about the things that your spouse is passionate about. This is one of the things we do as we become more united with our spouse. This is part of intimacy. I have grown to actually enjoy the game now and as our son Skyler grows in the sport, I can be seen as the loud, unruly mom shouting from the sidelines. Yes, that's me!

In order to appreciate it, I had to get closer to it. Now, because I'm closer to it (proximity), I'm supporting my son and loving what my husband loves (access) and we are engaged in doing this activity together (spending time). I also have now developed my own personal, intimate relationship with football. The truth is, it's not the sport but the intimacy with my husband that I love. My love for my son and my husband creates a pathway for me to love what they love.

[MJ] The flip side of that coin is that my wife loves chick flicks and dance films. I can bet the farm that if a wedding themed, J-Lo starring or estrogen-charged film surfaces, all systems are go! Also, any dance based movie (big or low budget, part 1, 2 or 6) is going to end up on our TV. The reality is, I don't care much for dance or damsels, but I do care much for my wife. Being close to her in proximity and appreciating what she loves is well worth the price of admission. The price of admission also provides front row seating and access to her heart, in addition to allowing me to fulfill my own love language of spending time. So if you think that may have been a tear trickling down my cheek, it's not because of the film; it's the chick that got me into the flick!

[KJ] Ironically, there are many similarities between our physical relationship with each other in marriage and our spiritual relationship with God. The same way I long to be close to my husband, be familiar with him, spend time with him, have a relationship with him and be intimate with him, God (our Father) desires the same intimacy with us as His children. He wants us to be familiar with Him, to spend time with Him, to be close to Him and to be in an intimate, purposeful and intentional relationship with Him. He desires us to be attentive to Him and aware of His presence. He wants us to be all in. Why? So we can learn to love better. When we are intimate with God, we become more like Him. He is the very definition of love. When we learn intimacy from our Heavenly Father, do we think that could impact our marriage? Certainly! If we can master the discipline of learning how to be intimate with our spouse, we will have conquered half the battle of experiencing the spiritual desire God has for us here in the physical.

[MJ & KJ] Intimacy is far more than just a physical relationship. It includes sex, but it's so much more than that. Relationships become so much more meaningful when there is intimacy involved. The closer we are to someone, the more mindful of his or her feelings, thoughts and wellbeing we become. Enjoying 20 years of marriage and sex, we confirm that God created it to be pleasurable and delightful. Similar to how the Holy Trinity has several functioning parts that all come together as one, sex was created so we could experience oneness with our spouse.

Is it any wonder why sex -- and the perversion of it -- is so high on the steal, kill and destroy agenda of the enemy? The enemy loves to pervert, twist and distort sex with the intent of making it something casual and matter-of-fact instead of something birthed from intimacy. It was designed to be exciting and enjoyable between two people within the protection and covering of the marriage covenant. Interestingly, before we were married we were constantly tempted beyond measure to do it, yet after we were married with full access to sex, we have to be convinced to want to do it. See the irony in that? Many couples experience the lure of sex that likens us to ravenous vegetarians seeking after forbidden fruit. Then, within the safety of marriage, God gives us the *entire garden,* yet we change our sexual appetites to now have carnivorous desires.

On the journey to becoming intimate in marriage, we sometimes have to deal with what's happened in the past. Some of the toughest issues we have to deal with when marriage counseling are rooted in each spouse's thoughts and expectations about sex. Those thoughts and expectations can be derived from having premarital sex, unhealthy relationships or experiencing some sort of perversion, misuse or abuse causing us to misunderstand our body in a sexual way. The good news is God knew everything we would all do (and everything that would be done to us) and preemptively sent His Son to counter our efforts to abandon His love for us. Everything sinfully done, after it's brought to him, is completely washed in the blood of Jesus. Not just covered but cleansed – meaning *wiped clean.*

We want to make sure that we address all the ways that we may have misused intimacy, so we don't miss out on one of God's greatest gifts that He designed to be enjoyed in the covenant and the intimacy of marriage. This means that even if we lost our virginity or it was taken away from us, through Christ we can regain our *purity*. We can be restored and whole again, physically, mentally, spiritually and sexually. If we don't talk about these things, we may be settling for less than what God has for us. So we implore you to communicate with your spouse about your thoughts about sex and intimacy.

[KJ] For example, when my husband and I were first married, we never went to premarital counseling. I think if we had gotten some wise Christian counseling, it could have saved us a lot of heartache. One of the things that we never discussed (and to be honest, I never discussed with anyone, ever) was that I was molested as a child. Quite frankly, it was something that I had never spoken of until *seven years* into our marriage. One may say, "What does this have to do with you being intimate in your marriage?" *Quite a bit*. The childhood sexual abuse had become the foundation of what I thought about sex, intimacy and even how I felt about my own body. Therefore, it had everything to do with my marriage.

I believe many women and men reading this right now may have suffered some form of childhood sexual misuse and can not only personally relate to my story, but also may be experiencing symptoms of abuse in your own current marital situations. I don't think I realized just how much this childhood encounter would affect me into my adulthood and not just on a conscious level. The molestation actually affected my subconscious level and controlled my thoughts about sex.

I was molested at the age of 11, and it left me feeling very dirty and shameful. Consequently, my first sexual encounter left me feeling dirty and shameful. Thereafter, any kind of sexual activity brought up these feelings of guilt and shame. When sexual encounters would occur outside of marriage, I would always revert back to the little molested girl; guilty, ashamed, dirty and victimized. I didn't like the way it made me feel, so I would try to avoid sex and intimacy at all costs. Something I never shared with anyone until I was an adult was suppressed for many years and facilitated my dysfunctional thoughts and feelings about love, sex and intimacy.

These feelings regarding sex would carry over into my marriage. The very place where sex and intimacy should be beautiful and free would carry the same discomfort as though it were a shameful act. What was the result?

Ultimately, this experience would end up keeping me from climaxing and experiencing orgasm during the first seven years of my married life. *I had never experienced it, so I never knew what I was missing.* Our mind does crazy things to protect us from harmful thoughts or traumatic experiences, so I didn't even realize all the emotions and feelings I had suppressed for all those years. It kept me from being completely intimate with my husband without even knowing it.

During another different yet traumatic experience later in my life, these memories came flooding back. As I finally dealt with them and sorted them out with God, I began to process what happened and realized that I had been withholding my emotions, my thoughts and my body from my husband. Once I overcame this obstacle, everything changed for the both of us. Our intimacy, our sex life and our relationship exploded...literally! It was brand-new, exciting and full of passion. It was free and beautiful. It was honorable in His eyesight. Intimacy with your spouse can create a passion and a love that is inexplicable. The truth is, unlike what we've been told in the media, a good marriage and true sexual intimacy takes a lot of work. It's important to remember that men communicate differently than women; this is also true as it relates to sex. Both men and women desire sexual intimacy, physically, emotionally and spiritually yet both genders must remain aware that we are wired differently.

Now, in the famous words of hip hop artists Salt N' Pepa, *Let's Talk about Sex.*

GPS (Godly, Purposeful Sex)

[MJ & KJ] If we learn and study each other and seek to understand each other, we will understand the inherent differences between men and women. Men view sex as a primary need: air, water, food, sex (and not necessarily in that order)! Men often view sex as a physical event and are ready for it at any time. They're stimulated by what they see; it's easy for a man to become aroused. It is essential for a man to climax and being naked is often part of it for him. Men are visual. This may be a revelation to some men, but there is a difference between ejaculation and orgasm. Many men can become satisfied with just the release of their bodily fluids, yet never reach the mental stimulation and even spiritual connectivity of climax when all senses are engaged, including the spirit. The truth is that God desires to be with us, even in our bedrooms. This is the embodiment of what becoming one flesh should look and feel like.

Unlike men, women often view sex as a secondary need. They look at sex in regard to relationship, and how they feel is stimulated by emotion. Women are aroused by emotion and are typically stimulated audibly. We often joke about how an unattractive man can have a gorgeous wife and wonder, "How did that happen?" *The gift of gab*. Women respond to what they hear. Many women may have experienced being enamored by the wrong man who was saying the right things.

For many women, orgasms are optional and sometimes random, depending on the patience and due diligence executed by a husband who is not just out "to get his." Husbands, it's what you say that can get you there, but it's what you do that can get her there. Wives are aroused by servant hood and it may take some time to arrive at a place where they are "ready." Ever heard the saying,

"Anything worth having is worth waiting for"? Husbands, apply generously if needed.

Many of our thoughts about sex inside of marriage are derived from some twisted thought process we've learned incorrectly outside of marriage. Casual sex is never simply just a physical act. Entering into a sexual relationship outside of marriage with the intent of "no strings attached" doesn't address the creation of "soul ties." Sadly, *many have exchanged strings for ties.* These soul ties are the previous sexual relationships and experiences our souls are connected to and can exist between people, images, acts, masturbation and anything we become intimate with outside of the marriage covenant, a place where sex and intimacy were designed and intended to be safe.

God intended sex to be a deep, spiritual action between a husband and wife coupled in marriage. If we have engaged in sex outside of these confines, typically there's baggage that comes along with it. We will have to submit all of those things to the Lord and to one another, and He can restore us back to what He originally intended for us to experience as a married couple. God is glorified when we seek to please our spouse. He is glorified when we overcome barriers and past hurts and discuss our sex lives. He is glorified when we fulfill our spouse's needs and help them experience pleasure and delight that He designed and intended exclusively for married couples. God is glorified when we go low and prefer our spouse over ourselves (no pun intended, but appropriate).

Married Forever writers Anthony and Phyllis Breech, a resource provided by Victory World Church provides an additional listing of Sexual Differences between Men and Women on pages 92-96. This is a great resource you may consider using that may be found at www.victoryatl.com.

It's important that we learn what our spouse prefers and not feel like we know everything without asking. It's much easier to arrive at the destination when you know exactly where you're going. Seek to have Godly, pleasurable sex. **G**odly, **p**urposeful **s**ex. GPS. God invented sex, purposed it inside of us and He wants us to enjoy it within the parameters of marriage. Our bodies are not our own, meaning our bodies belong to our spouse. When we are given marital instruction by the Lord to submit to one another, He doesn't just say these things to say them; He says them so we have a template to work from. A blueprint. When we are truly intimate with our spouse, it can shield us from trying to meet our needs outside of our marriage.

It's important that we communicate openly and honestly with each other every day. When this is happening, it will keep us in tune with each other. Ladies, we will know his physical needs – and men, we will know her emotional needs and vice versa. Typically, when a man looks for affection outside of the marriage, it can be traced back to a lack of intimacy with his wife. When a woman looks for affection outside of a marriage, it can often be traced back to lack of affection, attention or conversation. A blueprint is provided to avoid any additions to our marital homes without approval from the architect, the author and finisher of our lives together in marriage. Think of the Holy Spirit as the building inspector. He won't be approving any outside modifications that may damage the integrity of our marital structure.

Another thing that builds intimacy in marriage is *praying together*. When we pray with our spouses, we get to hear their most intimate thoughts and concerns that they share with the Lord.

Make Love, Not War

[KJ] It's important that we never use sex as a weapon. When we are angry or frustrated we should not withhold our body as ransom, male or female. It sends the wrong message to our spouses, and it makes them feel as if our love is conditional. Make sure that our sex lives and the intimacy between us is a priority. Simplified, if we don't make intimacy a priority, it won't be a priority. Just like we schedule vacations, practices, lunch meetings or anything else in life, we must make a special effort to include intimacy into the schedule as well. Ultimately, our spouse is the most important relationship here on earth, and it's important for us to act like it. The beauty happens when this action becomes a learned behavior, and the act is no longer required. The act is replaced by the action, and a natural desire to regularly satisfy each other is achieved.

One of the things to keep in mind is that *preparation is key*. In order to keep the intimacy alive in our marriage, we have to work at it. My spouse and I came up with a system called "foreplay at four." It's where we intentionally engage in at least four points of contact during the day as preparation for a night of intimacy. Whether that is a note, call, text, Facebook message, e-mail, kiss, hug, caress, tender words, longing gazes, charming advances or dirty talk, we try to initiate these things to give the heads up of where our heads are at for the evening. There's no law or instruction that anyone must do this. This is just a personal practice we instituted that works for us. You may require five-play at five or sex-play at six... for you and your spouse it may take more or less preparation earlier in the day to initiate expectations for later in the evening. This is just something we put in place to strive towards becoming more in tune with each other's needs/desires, and we wanted to share. Through this "foreplay at four" technique, he is preparing her mentally and she is preparing physically; we have found this to be a healthy way to sexually and sensually communicate with each other.

Stay Creative

[MJ & KJ] It is essential to keep it fresh and not just repeat the same old things. It's no different than if you eat chicken every meal, every day for years. How long do you think it will take before you are bored with it? It's important to keep it fresh and lively. We must use our creativity to spice things up a bit. We encourage wives to become your husband's fantasy. Fantasies are a good thing if your thoughts and fantasies are about your spouse. We encourage you to share with one another what your pleasures, desires and fantasies are. If you can't tell your spouse, you can't tell anyone, right? We encourage husbands to be your wife's knight in shining armor, the focal point of her affections.

We are often asked what is allowed or permitted in regards to sex. The word says *"Marriage is honorable among all, and the bed undefiled," (Hebrews 13:4, NKJV).*

The scripture goes on to instruct that fornication and adultery will be judged by God, yet what a married couple does together within the covenant of marriage seems to be given a moral flexibility for a couple to determine what is acceptable and pleasurable together between husband and wife. There should be a spiritual element involved in this decision-making process so that the lines of pleasure and perversion don't get mistakenly crossed. That being said, we should all have some boundaries established so that our spouse feels safe with us. We have personally incorporated these five questions in order to determine if it's something we should try.

1. Does it increase our oneness or intimacy together?

Couples often inquire if it is ok to have sex toys, gadgets or pornography to accompany them in the bedroom for added pleasure and stimulation. The word does not have a direct answer of this question, yet we would suggest if the object in question decreases the connectivity between the husband and wife, even if adding pleasure, then the dependency on the object or act takes the place of the intimacy between the husband and wife and may be considered questionable. This is not to create a list of do's and don'ts. This simply means if what you as a couple are seeking to do will increase intimacy and oneness, the creator of intimacy and oneness will probably be in agreement with it. Men are visual. Adding porn into the equation is allowing other people to visually enter the sanctity of the bedroom. Women are audio. Sounds of sexual interaction with other people for stimuli intrude on the personal objective of two people becoming one. Porn does not increase oneness, and therefore, we highly recommend against it.

2. Is it truly pleasurable or agreeable?

We should spend a lifetime learning our spouse. We develop, grow and mature. Exploration of creativity, positions, likes and dislikes are encouraged within the covenant of marriage.

3. Is it hygienically and physically safe?

Is it okay to use lubricants or gels to enhance pleasure? We are not sex therapists or doctors. We have been married and having sex together for 20 years, and from personal experience, we can suggest whatever you agree upon as husband and wife should be hygienically and physically safe.

4. Can I do this with a clear conscience before God?

We believe God created intimacy to be a beautiful, pleasurable and spiritually uniting experience. It's the expression of two people becoming one together in spirit. When this is the result of our intimate relationship with our spouse, we believe our Father is pleased.

5. Is it something I would want my own children to practice in their marriage someday?

We seek our sexual relationship in marriage to be fulfilling but not filthy, pleasurable not perverted, sensual not sinful, loving not lustful, and climactic not condemning. We desire the Lord to be glorified in every area of our lives and into the lives of our children. Leaving a family legacy of healthy, intimate relationships throughout our generation begins with us. Cutting off soul ties, perverted sexual acts and instituting appropriate sexual behaviors into our lives become a part of our spiritual DNA.

We determined that if we can answer all of those questions with a "yes," then we have agreed to proceed. *This is what personally works for us.* We encourage others to prayerfully seek to develop Godly guidelines to assist you in navigating your intimate lives together. God desires to bring pleasure into marriage that we humanly can't provide and manufacture on our own. When we allow our manly physical and womanly mental to collide with His Godly spiritual... Boom.

We believe intimacy is a key building block for a successful marriage. It is a cornerstone or foundational rock upon which to stack our other life goals. Next to God, we were intended to be the closest person to our spouse. Jesus desires to love us more deeply, more intensely. The Lord desired to be closer to your spouse, so He gave him or her *you*. To love your spouse more intimately, He needs *your* body to work through. Are you making yourself available to God to love your spouse how he or she needs and desires to be loved? One of the most powerful things that God revealed to us about each other is that we are God's hands here on earth. We are Christ's hands in action. When He desires to be closer to us, to walk beside us and hold our hand, He uses the hands of our spouse. When He desires to pull us close to give us a loving embrace, He uses the arms of our spouse. When comforting us with a Godly shoulder to cry on, He provides the shoulders, chest and heartbeat of a spouse. He has given us all the power to heal our spouse from fleshly desires, and this is the gift of healing hands. God will equip us for intimacy with our spouse if we ask Him and commit to losing ourselves to gain His more detailed plan for healthy intimacy. If we are diligent and consistent, it will work.

Here are a few more thoughts to consider regarding intimacy:

Whatever it took to get them, it takes to keep them: We cannot forget the art of courting and dating our spouse; even after marriage, the rules still apply. Stay in good health and well groomed. Continue to date your mate. Being mindful of our appearance is important and may add to the potency of the relationship. Work towards keeping your spouse's desire for you. We may even pray that we remain desirable to our spouse and that we remain active and fruitful.

Date night is imperative! This is not an option; it is a requirement! If we don't take time together, it is easy to be distracted. Life can and will get in the way and disrupt communication with the person who is supposed to be closest to us. Date night keeps our communication flowing and the passion alive. If we don't spend time investing in our marriage, it will take a backseat to all the other issues and activities of life and our intimacy can easily become a casualty of war. Dating is a lifetime process! It never stops. We were designed to fall in and out of love over and over again, so we may experience the freshness and life-giving renewal of intimacy reignited. Dating is a part of that process. Ladies, remind him why he fell in love and what made him fall. Gentlemen, swoon her continually back into your arms where she may find she is safe in His arms. She will give her whole self to you when you give your whole self to Him. Did you get that? Also, don't allow budget restrictions to hinder your dating advances. There are tons of things we can do that cost almost nothing but are worth the world. Here are just a few ideas:

1. Writing each other love letters and reading them aloud in the bath with candles and background music. (When is the

last time we actually presented a handwritten letter or note to our spouse? An e-mail or text doesn't count!)

2. Simulate a power outage; sit by the fireplace or lit candles. Feed each other finger foods like chocolate dipped strawberries.

3. Put together a musical playlist (we used to call them "mix tapes" back in the day) of songs from special moments past and extraordinary moments to come to help create the soundtrack to our lives.

4. Purchase or pick flowers from the side of road, take her to a lookout place to view the stars and dream together.

5. Go to a coffee shop, park or quiet place with a dictionary and pick out words to describe your mate. Share them with each other. This can be done at home as well, over a candle-lit dinner. With intention, the simple efforts can become sensual experiences.

6. Surprise her or him with a night out or a home cooked meal.

7. Prepare a Radical Date Night. Take care of the detailed songs, card, and flowers. Plan everything to the smallest detail; write a letter or card telling her how much you appreciate her for her wisdom, knowledge, skills and hot body! Ladies, you may even pursue your husband and initiate the advances as a change of pace.

8. Read to each other as the sun goes down or up, depending on your schedule.

Examples: "Love and Respect" by Emerson Eggerichs or Songs of Solomon.

9. Write the story of how you met. Remind each other of the details of the marriage proposal or wedding day.

10. Use cell phone and camera photos and actually print them out and have them bound as a keepsake. The physical copy always adds a new dimension than just seeing them in a digital format.

11. Movie Marathon Night: Redbox = $1.50.   during the time of this writing. Popcorn = $4.   Cuddling with your honey = priceless [FYI: In the Jordan household, the actual term "marathon" requires three movies viewed as a minimum.]

12. Serve her or him breakfast in bed.

13. Go out for just coffee and dessert, no dinner. Or, go to dinner and start with dessert.

14. Put a change jar in the kitchen and save all change for three months. Agree to cash it in to go on a date, but you can only spend what is in the jar.

15. Kiss or dance in the rain.

16. Picnic in the park or in your room.

17. Backyard moonlight dinner under the stars.

18. Dance to old records in your living room. Dance together. Dance for each other.

19. Have a water fight or food fight.

20. Shower or bathe together.

21. Drive around and get lost on purpose.

22. Hold hands and go for a walk.

23. Initiate peaceful touch. Not all massages need to be sexual. Brush or wash each other's hair.

24. Work out together.

Remember that our marriage is our #1 ministry and the most important relationship here on earth. Marriage is a lifetime investment. Most of the things we spend our time on are fleeting or passing. We won't remember most of life's insignificant occurrences a year from now, a month from now and possibly even moments from now. However, the special moments we create and experience with our spouses produce memories that last a lifetime. These moments are worth the investment of time.

Never Stop Learning

[MJ] As couples, we must take the time to learn about each other. We must study each other. I am still learning new things about my wife, 20+ years in. It excites me that there is still more to know. One of the greatest errors we can make in life is assuming we've got someone all figured out. How can we have completely figured out someone whom God is constantly changing?

[KJ] Throughout life, we take time to learn and study subjects like work charts, graphs, the solar system, calendars, sports, career requirements and technological advancements, just to name a few. What would happen if we devoted the same effort and energy into learning about our spouse? What if we continually tried to gain a deeper understanding of what makes them tick or the things that are important to them? What things are on their bucket list? (A bucket list is a list things to do before you die.) Taking the time on a date night to explore some of these things will give us tons of material to work from and towards as we move forward in this quest of intentional intimacy with our spouse. As an incentive, we included the list of "a few of my favorite things" from my husband and me at the end of this chapter. We also included a blank "a few of my favorite things" list for you and your spouse to fill out. Sounds like a perfect date night activity.

I often think about what it will be like when I stand before the Lord; what will He say? I'm certain he will ask me lots of things. The one thing I want to make sure of as I prepare for that day is that he is pleased with how I treated His son.

As promised, here are my responses:

A Few of My Favorite Things
Kristin Shai Jordan
Favorite Color: Purple
Love Language: Acts of Service
Favorite Vacation Spot: Maui, Hawaii
Still Want to Visit: Fiji

Number: 25

Favorite Dessert: Dark Chocolate

Favorite Restaurant: Ray's on the River, GA

Favorite Thing to do: Travel with my family

Favorite Movie: My Best Friend's Wedding

Favorite Song: "Let's Stay Together" by Al Green

Favorite Holiday: Christmas

Favorite Flower: Sterling Silver Roses

Favorite Board Game: Yahtzee or Scrabble

Favorite Thing about Spouse: Kindness and gentleness

Favorite Memory: Hanging with my husband in Mexico

Favorite Bible Verse: John 15:7

Favorite Quote: "When people show you who they are, believe them" –Maya Angelou

Most Important Lesson Learned: Forgive everyone of everything

Thing I Wish I Could Change: All of my family would come to know Christ and live for Him

How I would like to be Remembered: Wise and loving

My husband's responses:

A Few of My Favorite Things

Montell Du'Sean Jordan

Color: Crimson red

Love Language: Quality time and touch.

Favorite Vacation Spot: Anywhere my wife is! Specifically, Hawaii, Australia, or with the family in Orlando

Still Want to Visit: Thailand and China

Favorite Number: 4 or 9

Favorite Dessert: Key Lime Pie (Mrs. Polly Byrnes')

Favorite Restaurant: Hugo's Cellar (The 4 Queens Hotel, Las Vegas, NV)

Favorite Thing to Do: Movie marathons with my wife and vacations with my family

Favorite Movie: Harlem Nights (Eddie Murphy)

Favorite Song: Ready Or Not (After 7)

Favorite Holiday: Christmas

Favorite Flower: Red Carnation

Favorite Board Game: Monopoly

Favorite Thing about Spouse: She knows me better than anyone else, other than God.

Favorite Memory: Mexico/Guacamole and a near death experience while creating life (I'll leave you wondering!)

Favorite Bible Verse: Philippians 4:8-9

Favorite Quote: "When there is no hope for the future, there is no power in the present." –John Maxwell

Most Important Lesson Learned: The truth, when not told in love, won't be received.

Thing I Wish I Could Change: Improper use of finances earlier in my career

How I Would like to be Remembered: A faithful husband, dedicated father, and man of God who loved the world enough to point them towards Jesus.

Now it's your turn. Print a copy of this for you and your spouse. Fill them out together. Discuss them and share them. Learn from them. This is not a quiz. It's supposed to be fun and allow your spouse to hear directly from you. Enjoy each other!

A Few of My Favorite Things

Name:

Favorite Color:

Love language:

Favorite Vacation spot:

Still want to visit:

Favorite Number:

Favorite Dessert:

Favorite Restaurant:

Favorite Thing to do:

Favorite Movie:

Favorite Song:

Favorite Holiday:

Favorite Flower:

Favorite Board Game:

Favorite Thing about Spouse:

Favorite Memory:

Favorite Bible Verse:

Favorite Quote:

Most important lesson learned:

Thing I wish I could change:

How I would like to be remembered:

CHAPTER 15

Overcoming Trial & Tragedy

[MJ & KJ] This is probably one of the weightiest and most important topics we will cover within these pages. A preacher once said "Either you are in the midst of a storm, coming out of a storm or preparing to go into one." Unfortunately, this is a life truth that is only magnified in marriage. The word of God doesn't instruct us that trouble will possibly arise in our lives; it assures us it will definitely come. Our marriages are not exempt from these storms, yet the covering of marriage can be a refuge during the time of trials and tribulation. The most important part of weathering a storm is learning how to navigate the waters to safely come out on the other side of it.

All the days of our marriages will not be rosy or anywhere near perfect; this is simply a reality. In the context of our blueprint, this means we may anticipate there will be structural damage to our marriage. The saving grace is that Jesus provides us with an infallible insurance that guarantees we may overcome any and every circumstance the enemy hurls at us, as long as we receive the policy. It is during the early process of building our foundation that testing is needed to make sure the marriage is structurally solid to carry the weight of later life experiences that will arise. We are aware no one wants to go into marriage thinking about these things, but truthfully, these are the things that often become the defining moments of a marriage. Our challenges can actually make marriage stronger if we learn how to handle situations in faith, not fear. We can never truly know how durable our marriages are and how faithful our God is until tested. There is no testimony without the *test*.

Sadly, during the difficult seasons of life, many couples may find themselves facing each other in battle formation rather than taking the posture of a unified front entering into battle together. Keep in mind, soldiers in the same company don't face each other when going into battle; they stand side by side. This is how we face our opponent. Rather, in times when we are surrounded on every side (this is how the enemy often unfairly attacks marriages), we have learned that standing back-to-back makes overcoming the opposition coming against us a much easier battle. Knowing that someone has your back in the tough times is critical. It takes courage to face trials and tribulations head on, but this doesn't mean that we won't be afraid. Peter walked on water, but he was probably scared senseless! Courage is facing the trial in the face of fear. The same way Peter walked on the sea while focused on the creator of the sea, we too can navigate the stormy waters of life with our spouse while remaining focused on Christ. He becomes a lighthouse to us in the midst of uncertain waters to help navigate us back to safety. In the storm, we have the choice to panic or be at peace. How we behave in a crisis, in the midst of a storm, can define our marriage.

We begin by submitting to you that tragedy does not come from God. Do you understand that? *Tragedy does not come from God*! The voice in your head may be saying, "But what about Job?" When we think about the biblical story of Job, his name alone brings up visuals of great loss, suffering and tragedy. However, if we look deeper beneath the surface of the story, we actually discover that God was *bragging* on Job. God honored Job. Satan, the enemy, was Job's designated accuser. Satan argued to God that the reason Job was honorable was because he had it made, living the good life. God placed a hedge of protection around him. The enemy suggested that if all of Job's material possessions, family blessings and health were taken away, he would surely curse God to His face. The enemy suggested that Job was faithful to God for what God had done, and not for who God is. God took Satan up on proving Job's faithfulness. The tests or trials were allowed to come relentlessly from the enemy himself.

[MJ] Why would God allow such a thing to happen? Why would a good, loving, kind, gracious God remove His hand of protection and provision and allow tragedy to befall Job, *His* faithful servant?

For that matter, why would he allow it to happen to you or me? *So that He can get glory.*

Two things immediately come to mind. First, there is a biblical occurrence that documents a man who had been blind from birth who encountered Jesus.

> *Now as Jesus passed by, He saw a man who was blind from birth. And His disciples asked Him, saying, "Rabbi, who sinned, this man or his parents, that he was born blind?" Jesus answered, "Neither this man nor his parents sinned, but that the works of God should be revealed in him." John 9:1-3 (NKJV)*

This illustration shows us that many circumstances that we face are not the product of our sin, disobedience or a genetic curse of God's wrath. Many times the circumstance or occurrence is so that God's glory may be seen.

I went on my very first mission trip to Nicaragua in March of 2014. I have traveled all over the world many times and filled over two passports with destination stamps, entering and exiting nations. However, in 45 years of life, this was my first time traveling to serve God rather than to receive from Him.

During this journey, I was able to see an impoverished and destitute portion of a third-world society that was unimaginable. While being hosted by friends Mike and Debra Turner with a ministry known as Life Link International, www.lifelinkint.org, I was able to witness during a vision walk a plea from a parent who sought to get her eight-year-old daughter, a straight-A student, admitted into their already overcrowded private school. This school was like a paradise or a mini-oasis in the middle of chaos. The small slice of Heaven on Earth for the kids admitted into this school included education, a uniform, clean water and a meal and snacks throughout the day, prior to returning to their dirt floor abodes. By day's end, this little girl had all those things, including a sponsor who committed to contributing a monthly fee to secure her enrollment. She was scheduled to start school the very next day. Christ used one of us to be His hands in action here on the earth. She was born there under extreme circumstances. God met her there and then sometimes uses you and me to perform His miracles.

The next thing that came to mind may actually mess with your theology a bit. There is an account in scripture when Jesus instructs his disciples, after a long day of ministry, to get onto the boat and head to the other side of the lake. Watch what happens in this turn of events:

> *Immediately Jesus made His disciples get into the boat and go before Him to the other side, while He sent the multitudes away. And when He had sent the multitudes away, He went up on the mountain by Himself to pray. Now when evening came, He was alone there.*

But the boat was now in the middle of the sea, tossed by the waves, for the wind was contrary. Matthew 14:22-30 (NKJV)

In this instance, Jesus *made* the disciples get on the boat to meet Him on the other side of the lake. One must consider that as He is the Son of God -- He certainly knew the storm was coming. He sent them anyway. *He knowingly sent the disciples into a storm.* The important thing to remember is that although He sent them, He also met them there in the midst of the storm and made sure they made it through safely. They also got to witness a miracle while in the storm that they otherwise would have never experienced on dry land. Perhaps there is a miracle awaiting us in the storm we are in, coming out of or possibly entering into. We may be assured that He will meet us there and is faithful to see us through to the other side. Many of the disciples were highly skilled fisherman and they spent their time on the water. Surely they noticed the weather conditions (for the wind was contrary) and suggested alternative travel dates for Jesus, their travel agent, to consider when booking on their behalf. Yet, they were all present. We too must be willing to get on the boat and sometimes even walk on water.

[KJ] I don't know about you but in my life, there have been seasons where I felt like those disciples navigating their way across the stormy seas. I even felt like I had Job-like obstacles. If we are not careful, focusing on our problems more than God's promises can create a question of doubt in our minds whether God really is with us and for us. Regardless of how long or how difficult our trial may be, we need to keep in mind that God can turn it around in the blink of an eye, the snap of a finger or the calming of a sea. One of the things that blows my mind when I read the book of Job is that there are 42 chapters where Job is tested and tried; it only takes five verses of one chapter to undo everything that happened to him in those lengthy previous 42 chapters! It's how we handle the tragedy and the trial that play a huge role in determining the outcome of our marriage.

Looking back and really assessing what Job did in the midst of his trial tells us a lot about him. In the midst of his trial, he worshiped, he blessed the Lord, he defended God, he covered his wife, he recounted the blessings of God, he praised God for who He is, he repented and prayed for forgiveness for what he may have done and he prayed for his friends. In the end, his blessings were restored, and he received double for his trouble. Even if you are at the beginning of your marriage and have not experienced any trials and tribulations, they will come. Just remember that trials are an opportunity for us to honor the Lord even in the midst of pain. If we are in the midst of trial, the Lord might be asking us to look into His eyes instead of the waves we actually see.

Now faith is the substance of things hoped for, the evidence of things not seen. Hebrews 11:1 (NKJV)

The word says our faith is *now*. So it's our faith, *now*, that will take us through trials and tribulations. I honestly have no idea how people make it in marriage or in life without the Lord. During every life difficulty we've endured, it was our hope and faith in God that helped us to keep going and not give up. It is our hope and our prayer that through our transparency of our personal testimonies in this book, many would find some truth that would penetrate the heart and resonate within the spirit. It is the countless struggles that we've overcome that allow us the opportunity to even share with you today. We have achieved victory in Christ, and you can too!

I'd like to share part of our testimony with you to keep you encouraged and remind you there's nothing that God can't fix. Many may be thinking that your circumstance is different from ours and that we may not understand what you've been through. Even in our personal, unique circumstances, Jesus's saving and transformational power may be applied to us all. There's nothing that's beyond God's redemption. Over the next few paragraphs, allow me to share part of our testimony in hopes you may find a little bit of your story in ours.

There was a seven-year period of time where I felt very similar to Job. Each morning, I didn't want to get out of bed for fear of what awaited me that day. During this season of time we will refer to as "the dark period," every day was a challenge. During the dark period we battled infidelity and experienced the betrayal of close and seemingly faithful friends. Our record company business failed, and during the process of losing everything, including all our employees and our office, we would also lose our musical catalog, including nearly 15 years of intellectual property. This storm all occurred as we stood on the brink of bankruptcy, literally $1.7 million in debt. These waters went from ankle to waste deep to barely being able to tread water. We felt like we were drowning.

Seven lawsuits, all our monies being withheld, the loss of a child, our home burning to the ground, the repossession of a car, and like Job, while this news was happening, even more bad reports came. Our finance was levied and properties leaned, our credit was destroyed and we even experienced having "a hit" put on us while disputing a family situation. Add to all this, we accumulated church hurt (feelings of manipulation in ministry), family members turning against us, the loss of a music career and record deal, topped with depression and a cherry on top called sickness. This list is not all-inclusive by any means; these are just the highlights!

Most days during the dark period, I was afraid of what that day might hold. To the point of feeling like Job when he asked God to please take his life, I felt like I had had enough. Through each and every instance we would experience, the constant theme was the Lord saying, "It is not about you. I will give you double for your trouble." He would hold our hand through each trial previously listed and give us glimmers of hope to keep us moving forward. While each of these situations carried an enormous amount of stress and burden, I would like to share the specifics of one storm that tested our faith tremendously.

In 2005 we were celebrating our oldest son Christopher's 16th birthday and my dad's 60th. We were preparing a birthday dinner for both. We were excited to have my parents visiting from California. Just the night before, Montell had completed writing his autobiography that had taken nearly two years to complete and he was finally finished. I read it around 3 a.m. that morning, and I was extremely proud of him. He placed it on the edge of my desk in the front office of our home, where most of our other intellectual and creative properties like movie scripts, children's books we had written and illustrated and other documents were stored.

The plan that day was for me to prepare the meal at our home and take it to my aunt's house, where we would have the party. On a typical day like this I would normally get up and prepare the food and then go and get ready for the day. On this day, for some strange reason, I decided to switch it up. I got ready for the day thinking that I would almost finish getting dressed but put on my new shirt and my shoes later. Next, I went downstairs to prepare tacos for the party. I was cooking the meat on the stove in the kitchen when I looked up and saw something orange out of the corner of my eye. When I fully turned my head towards the back of the house, I saw *the entire rear of our home was on fire.* No alarms were sounding, and there was no warning of any kind because the fire was still on the outside of the house!

My heart was filled with terror. I began to look for my boys. Chris was with my younger son Skyler, who was 18 months old at the time, and I did not know where they were. My parents were taking a shower, and so I began to yell, "Get out! Get out of the house, it's on fire!" My parents came running butt-naked from the shower (which may have scarred me in other ways), and they began to scramble for their clothes to help me locate my boys. I was screaming their names at the top of my lungs. As I ran outside they were happily playing basketball together in the driveway on the side of the house and had no idea that there was a fire in the backyard that was already burning our house to the ground.

I instructed them to go across the street to our neighbor's house and wait there. I then grabbed the phone and called 911. Montell had taken our daughter Sydney to a rehearsal earlier that day and was returning home with the birthday cakes unaware of the blazing inferno that was now our home. I called my husband and exclaimed, "Baby! The house is on fire! Come home!"

In total shock he said, "What do you mean, on fire?"

I frantically replied, "*Like TLC on fire!*" He knew exactly what I meant. (Referring to when Lisa "Left Eye" Lopez of famous R&B group TLC burned down Andre Rison's home in 1994). I couldn't think of any other description to describe the magnitude of what I was looking at. Montell was doing about 95mph on the 85 freeway to get home.

Next, I called my pastors who lived just around the corner. When they quickly arrived with a fire extinguisher in hand, they realized they might have underestimated my explanation of "The roof is on fire." My children and parents were inside my neighbor's house as my pastors and I sat out in front of my house awaiting the fire fighters. I sat there feeling hopeless and in utter shock of what I saw transpiring before my very eyes. Our next-door neighbor came out to console me as we sat watching my roof ablaze. Finally, the firefighters showed up on the scene and hooked up their hoses to the hydrants, only to realize that because we lived in a fairly new subdivision, the pressure was too low and it would not generate sufficient water to the hoses. They notified the city immediately, yet we had to wait another 25 minutes for the water pressure to be adjusted as our house continued to burn to the ground. In my mind, I remembered Montell sitting his autobiography on my desk earlier that very morning, and I was instantly overwhelmed by a greater fear than the fire. It was the fear that my husband would suffer more loss of himself than the destruction happening right before me.

The firefighters were profusely apologizing as we stood there waiting. Soon the wind began to blow, and the trees in the backyard caught fire, which began to creep towards the house next door. Our loving and concerned neighbor, who had originally come to console me, was now in the same predicament as me. As you can well imagine, his tune and tone changed when it was his own house on fire. He began screaming at the firemen to help him fix it, but all we could do was sit and wait on the city.

As I stood there in front of this blazing inferno I can remember crying out to God, asking, "Why is this happening to us?" I told Him, "God, you know I live for you and I walk with you. How could this happen to me?" Huge tears streamed down my face as I felt hopeless and helpless. The longer I stood there, I more I cried out to God saying, "I don't understand!" I remembered at just that moment the irreplaceable items in my office: the freshly illustrated children's books, movie scripts and autobiography my husband had just finished. We were about five years into the dark period, and to say that it had been overwhelming would be an understatement. I knew that my husband would not be able to bear losing all of those things. They were originals and they didn't exist anywhere else but right there in that burning house. I began to cry out to God telling Him, "I need to see your hand today like never before. I don't know how you're going do it, but my husband cannot handle losing all that he has created and worked on for the last three years." That would be a tipping point for my husband and I knew it.

Despite what I saw, I began crying out and thanking God in advance! I needed God to show up like never before, and I was desperate! All I could see around me was chaos and pandemonium, but I could hear nothing. As the third house caught on fire, it was like a scene out of a bad movie. The horror of it all felt overwhelming. At just that moment, I turned my head to the left and saw my husband running up the street toward me. Even though authorities attempted to stop him from entering our neighborhood, he slipped past an officer. I ran and collapsed into his arms and melted deep into his chest, sobbing uncontrollably. He started asking me what happened. I told him all that I knew.

Just then, the water pressure came on and the firefighters began to hose down the houses on each side of our house. They were trying to contain the fire because it had spread from house to house now, as three houses were now fully ablaze. They apologized profusely for not being focused on our house, but they would have to sacrifice our house so that they could save the rest of the neighborhood from burning down. My heart sank; I knew that meant that there was no hope for our home.

As we stood on the lawn outside our neighbor's house across the street, the CNN and other media helicopters began to circle. The news reporters were also on their way up the hill at this point. I told my husband to go inside so we could avoid being on the six o'clock news. The dark period we had been in was hard enough on its own. It didn't need to be televised. My husband watched the blaze from the front window of the neighbor's living room.

We sat there for hours, which seemed like an eternity, watching the firefighters put out the two houses beside ours. Ours was still on fire as the gas heater burned from the basement. The prayer both of us were silently praying was, "God, please show us your hand." A neighbor who happened to be a photographer began taking photos from the beginning stages of this event until the completion, much later that evening.

The Red Cross showed up on the scene and they were extremely helpful and kind, and for that, I will always be grateful. The firefighters stayed all night long to make sure that nothing sparked any further. Three houses were seemingly completely destroyed. By evening's end, bulldozers came and completely demolished the other two houses beside ours. They didn't touch ours. Strangely, there had been a small portion of the front office area of our home and a portion of the garage that was still somehow intact, and therefore due to the possibility of it being salvageable and needed for review for insurance purposes, it was allowed to remain overnight.

We left and went to my aunt's house, where we had to face the questions of my then nine-year-old daughter, whom we had attempted to shield from being at the site and from watching the spectacle on television. I felt broken, defeated, consumed and overwhelmed. Having no idea where we would go from there I can remember sitting in the bath sobbing, crying out to God, "Where were you? Why?"

In that still, small voice God said to me, "It's not about you and I will give you double for your trouble."

I screamed out, "What do you mean, 'It's not about me?' I walked out of the house with no ID, no money, no shoes, wearing only a red apron, jeans, a white T-shirt and cheetah slippers, and we have nothing! What do you mean it's not about me?" I cried for what seemed like hours until I passed out.

The next day, my thoughts were consumed by questions. Now what? Where would we go? What would we do? There were so many questions, but not a lot of answers.

[MJ] The miracle would be revealed the following day. As we returned to the scene the next morning, the fire department met us to survey what remained of our home before confirming the completion of the demolition. We had been praying for a miracle but more specifically, for God to show us His hand. We had asked the Lord to cover our creative and intellectual property as we sat and watched our house burn down. That is, all but the *front office area* of the structure.

When we arrived to the house, the front portion of our home stood the way the roof originally did. It looked almost like a church steeple; everything around it completely burned to the ground, including the two homes beside us, yet it was as though a hand literally protected that small front office portion of the home in a bubble. A firefighter placed a ladder through what remained of the front window and wedged it onto a desk that was in the rear of the only remaining room. He crawled through the window into what remained of our office and to our shock, retrieved our hard drive disks, our scripts and the children's book. They were unharmed. Some of the materials were sopping wet from the water, but nothing was damaged or lost. Even the children's book illustrations still remained in a cabinet, and when he pulled out the only original copy and handed it out the window, still in the Kinko's bag, only a small corner of the bag was slightly singed. It was as though it was about to catch fire but somehow did not. Even the autobiography, which had been placed on that very desk earlier that morning, was sopping wet yet intact, hardly touched by the fire. Actually, *it barely even smelled like smoke.*

After retrieving the last of our belongings, just like out of a movie, as he pulled his ladder out of the window, *the entire floor collapsed.* The firefighter turned to us and said, "You all must be living right, 'cause I've never seen anything like that!" The floor beneath the carpet separating that room from the basement had been completely destroyed. The carpet was being held together by only the staples on the wall, so although there was the appearance of a floor, the whole thing had actually burned out underneath. When he exited the room with our things, the desk, carpet and everything that remained in the room that should have been burned to a crisp and bulldozed with the other previously demolished houses, finally dropped into the smoldering basement to join the rest of the ashes. It literally looked as if a giant hand invisibly cupped that portion of our home and protected our very existence.

If you recall, I mentioned a small portion of the garage still remained. You will find it interesting that although everything we owned was completely consumed, somehow our family photo albums, wedding pics and baby pictures of all our children just so happened to be in that small portion of the garage that did not burn or suffer from water damage. We saw both fire and flood, yet God showed His faithfulness in an unforgettable way. In the midst of one of the biggest tragedies of our lives, God showed up and showed out. The miracle didn't stop there.

[KJ] After three days of staying with relatives, my husband woke up that morning and instructed me to get in the car. He said we were going to look for a house. I began to remind him of all the reasons why this didn't make any sense. We had no money and no ID, and really, we had no clue. He said, "Trust me, babe, I know the Lord will lead us." We began to drive as if the Holy Spirit, leading us into a brand-new neighborhood, was navigating us. He drove all the way back to the very last house in the neighborhood where a "for rent" sign hung in the front window. This was a brand new home, never lived in, with a *for rent* sign in the window. I sat there in awe, wondering how in the world there was a *for rent* sign in a brand new house in a brand new subdivision in the exact same district where my children went to school. We called the number on the sign, and they said that they would meet us within the hour.

Immediately upon their arrival, the man walked directly inside the home and took the "for rent" sign out of the window. The woman with him turned to us and to our astonishment, said that the Lord had told them we were coming. This little Hispanic couple happened to be pastors. The Lord had them purchase that property years prior as an investment property, but then told them not to sell it. He told them they were only to rent it, and that He would let them know who to rent it to. On the way over there, *He told them* that we were the ones for whom they had been waiting. So this brand new home had literally been sitting there, uninhabited, for years. Immediately when we called, they knew we were the ones.

We sat there in utter disbelief. My husband and I were completely shocked. We began to tell them that we had no money, no identification and we didn't know if or when the insurance would kick in. We had no deposit slips, check stubs or any way to show them proof of employment or that we were even capable of paying the monthly rent. They simply said it didn't matter and told us to meet them for dinner to sign the contract and get the keys.

Later that same evening, we met them at a Cracker Barrel (where they paid for our dinner) and we signed the leasing agreement without a credit check or even putting down a deposit. They just gave us the keys, just like that! Within 72 hours, we were moving into a brand new, fully furnished home located in the same school district where our children attended, as if nothing had ever happened.

We moved into our rental home and lived there for a season as our house was being rebuilt. During this time, our family became tighter than ever, as the trial had somehow brought us closer together. It was good knowing that even in the midst of the storm, the Lord was on our side.

The Lord did more than just show us the miracle of preserving our intangible things and providing a remarkable home for us to live in. Next, He answered the "God, why me?" question in the most astounding way.

About three months after our fire, there would be another tragedy. This time, we were not the ones who went head first into the actual storm. The world refers to it as *Hurricane Katrina*. My mentor in the music business called me from New Jersey and told me that she had over 300 family members who would be displaced because of the hurricane's destruction. She told me that her cousin, her husband and their children would be coming to Atlanta for refuge. They had lost everything, and she needed me to go and check on them.

[MJ] We went that night and met them at the hotel where they would be staying. I clearly recall looking into the eyes of this husband, father and business owner who was now seated before me in the hotel lobby, having lost everything. Their account of the storm's magnitude was unimaginable. We got them a hotel room and paid for about two weeks. We then gave them money for food and clothing, with no thought of repayment or a desire for thanks. We brought them resources, but more importantly, God used us to bring them hope.

Our friend had told them about our family's tragedy only a few months prior, so they knew we were truly empathetic. As a family, we were able to witness to another family who had just lost everything from a place of knowing that God was going to redeem them. We loved on them from a place of experience. Through our personal pain, we were able to present God's promise. He had made a way for us just a few months prior, so we assured them that He would do it for them as well. We could speak to them with certainty, authority and confidence from our personal tragedy and because of what we had just come through, they could receive the message of hope and believe that God was going to do it for them as well. If we had not experienced the fire, we would have never been able to help them make it through the flood. We may not have even been able to comprehend what they were going through.

[KJ] I remember that night as I was going to bed, the Lord whispered to me, *"I told you it wasn't about you."* We had looked into the eyes of a mother who was hopeless, and following us sharing our testimony with her, she felt like there was some glimmer of hope. This made the fire worth it all. There was nothing I could have said to her if I hadn't experienced that, and I told her if it was just for that moment right there with her, it was all worth it. I meant that from the depths of my soul. That night, I fell asleep for the first time understanding with certainty that, "It was not about me."

[MJ & KJ] The challenges we have faced in this lifetime have drawn us closer to each other, closer to our children and most importantly, closer to God. In the midst of tragedy, we may choose to run to God or run from Him. Each day we are all given that choice, and although we have no control over what we face, we do have control over our response to adversity. Every single day is a choice. We get to decide. Not choosing is actually choosing. We chose to keep fighting and keep believing, remembering that when everything seems out of *our* control, everything is in *His* control. This is truly the meaning behind the verse where He promises to work everything out for the good of those that love Him. There is something extremely important to remember in living out the promise of this passage of scripture:

> *And we know that all things work together for good to those who love God, to those who are the called according to His purpose. Romans 8:28 (NKJV)*

Many people claim to love the Lord, yet they are not living in the calling to *His purpose*. If we love the Lord yet we are answering the calling to *our own purpose*, all things will *not* work together for our good. This is the difference between "thy will be done" and "my will be done."

Trust that if we are answering His call for our lives in our marriages, God will be in control and is faithful to allow the situation to make us instead of break us! We will emerge stronger, wiser and better.

As we travel the country and meet different couples and discuss their various trials and turmoil, we realize the dark period that we endured was for His glory. The more husbands and wives we meet and the more real-life stories that become shared experiences, the more we realize all of the things that we personally endured helped build our testimony so that we can help more people. Our testimony becomes our strength, and somehow, God allows His strength in us to inspire and encourage others.

We know a friend who, after only a few years of marriage, suffered the loss of his wife, leaving him with twin kids to raise on his own. We also know of a pastor's wife whose husband passed unexpectedly after 20 years of marriage, leaving her to raise three teenagers on her own. My mom remarried and had her husband die tragically and unexpectedly. Recently, an admired pastor from our old church passed away of a heart attack while delivering a message during 11am Sunday morning service. These tragedies are unexplainable, yet somehow God will get the glory from their testimonies. His strength is made perfect in our weakness which, tragically, is good news! This means that when we are at the end of our rope, at our wit's end, and ready to throw in towel, God will throw the towel right back into the ring so that He may show himself strong and faithful to defend us.

As you read this, keep in mind that the trial that you're going through right now will be used to help someone else in the future. You can't go over, under or around it to secure a valid testimony. Stay the course and avoid taking marital shortcuts, attempting to accelerate the process. Microwaved marriages lack flavor; God wants to cook us up something from scratch. A good ol' heavenly, home-cooked marital meal is His desire for us. He wants you to come through it. This is the purpose to which He is calling us.

Many of us still may not find solace in the truth that none of us are here for ourselves, but the reality remains, "It's not about us." *It's honestly not about you.* We were designed, created and given life as a solution to help someone else.

> *There is no greater love than to lay down one's life for one's friends. John 15:13 (NLT)*

It is our prayer that in the midst of your personal tragedy, circumstances or trial, that you allow God to make you victorious. Let God turn your trial and tragedy into triumph. Pastor Dennis Rouse says, "We cannot be victims and victors at the same time." Whether the trial is self-inflicted, a mistake, a bad decision, an indiscretion, infidelity, adultery or an unforeseen situation like accidents, sickness, disease or even an unexpected death, God is more than able to deliver you out of them all. Great testimonies are birthed out of great tests. When God chooses you, like Job, to brag on your marriage, family, stewardship and faithfulness, be reminded that although the enemy will do his worst, he is no match for God's best.

We can't wait until the test is over to begin thanking God for the victory. The secret is that in the midst of a tragedy, right smack dab in the middle of our pain, we have to pray, worship, rejoice, and thank the Lord for who He is. It's one of the most difficult things to do, and this is why many often find themselves in dark periods longer than necessary. Even in the darkness, we must look to the light -- Jesus.

[KJ] Don't stop communicating with God or your spouse. Don't give in to the temptation to have a pity party. We cannot allow the situation to steal our hope. Jesus gives hope to the hopeless, life to the lifeless and worth to the worthless. He paid a price, making us priceless! Your life may hold the very hope that someone else needs to survive. They may not make it out without knowing that you made it out and how you did it. Therefore, you must make it through!

We have the choice to be overwhelmed or overjoyed. We have a choice every day to live our lives in faith or fear. One gives life, and the other leads to death. Choose life! Choose faith! In spite of the hurt and sorrow we may feel, we have to communicate to our spouses that they are our best friends and needed more than ever before, even if they are in some way responsible for the trial at hand. Remember, our trials in this life can be viewed as stumbling blocks or stepping-stones but from Heaven, our mountains look like molehills.

We admire those who have overcome some sort of tragedy or adversity; it's their tenacity that draws us to them. We may or may not know their full story, but it is very seldom one achieves significance without having been through something extremely difficult. Many of us will find our plight has purpose only after the fact.

Thankfully, Montell and I chose to walk it out. We would have never experienced the beauty in this life of marriage had we pushed the eject button and aborted the promise to avoid the process. This is where God promises to exchange our beauty for ashes. The most beautiful trees are pruned back to the most unattractive stumps in order to allow them to grow into the beautiful creation they are to be. We are no different, as our pruning process often comes through trial and tragedy. We are the branches and He is the vine. Even while being pruned through life's difficulties, He provides the blueprint for landscaping our marriages to determine how fertile our land is, how big the tree can grow and how much fruit it will produce.

[MJ & KJ] We want to share today that everything we have shared with you concerning what God has brought us through has been worth it. It has made us stronger, and although our testimony is not yours, your decision can be the same one we chose; trust God beyond your own understanding. We hope you are inspired to not give up so that you too may experience a restoration that becomes a light and lifeline for someone else's marriage.

We are humbled, awed and privileged to be able to share our lives with you. God continues to blow our minds and reminds us daily it's not about us, but about His love for you. Perhaps you are experiencing trial and tragedy or possibly reading this in hopes to avoid some of the pitfalls that we did. A wise couple may learn from the mistakes of others while the unwise (foolish) will learn it on their own. Here lies an opportunity to choose. We got to decide and so do you. We are living testimonies that there is nothing and no one He can't redeem.

We love hearing about people's testimonies of overcoming trials and tragedy. It's like fuel for our souls, and we find strength in knowing we are not standing alone. Others will believe and trust God like we did and live to see the fruits of their labor of love in honoring the covenant of marriage.

If you'd like to share your story with us, we'd love to hear about it! Please visit our website at www.marriagemasterpeace.com and tell us about your story. Consider sharing how you have come through your storm and focus on God's hand in the journey you have victory in or expect to experience.

CHAPTER 16

Affair-Proofing Your Marriage

"Even if you think you can stand up to temptation, be careful not to fall." 1 Corinthians 10:12 (CEV)

[MJ & KJ] The blueprint is nearly complete. The structure and foundation we have been building our marriages upon has become a solid, not sandy foundation. Quality materials have gone into the construction process, and our marriages have been furnished and fully insured by the promises of God. Although our vows fully protect our marital homes, like any good buyer, we can't forget the final walk-through; a final inspection to make sure the home is ready for habitation. We know, figuratively and in reality, that just like a new home, a marriage can shift as it settles on its foundation. We must take periodic walks around the marriage home to be on the lookout for cracks or leaks. This cannot be done by overlooking, passing by or minimizing the major life issues that could define our marriage.

We can't go around or run through this process. We must walk through it. These final passages were some of the most difficult to write, yet we feel the transparency provided in our testimony provides an encouragement and hope that anyone can have a successful, loving and healthy marriage, even after an affair. It is possible to walk through the fire and pass through without smelling like smoke.

[MJ] As I currently write this, Kristin and I are in the wake of a television show airing of "Unsung," where we transparently showed how our marriage was transformed and the impossible was made possible. I shared how my infidelity -- when outmatched by God's sovereignty -- produced security, and as a result, hundreds of requests have flooded in from husbands and wives asking my wife and me to save their marriages. Our hearts go out each time, as we know in the 44-minute well-documented program, not all the ministry topics were covered. Many people missed the idea that Kristin and I were recipients of Jesus' healing power, not the catalysts.

Our story and personal testimony, although in some ways it may be similar to yours, still remains *our* testimony. We know all people are uniquely, individually and wonderfully made. Although we are all different, His covenant remains the same yesterday, today and forever, and His promises apply to everyone submitted to the safety He provides within the covenant of marriage. Everyone.

We didn't save our marriage; Jesus did. Infidelity, secrets, guilt, shame, depression and unhappiness were all healed and restored by the love and power of the Father. So if you are blessed to have never encountered this magnitude of storm in your personal marriage, take note of the do's and don'ts and use wisdom to navigate from our mistakes (experience). If you have weathered an adulterous storm (or are currently in the midst of one), please know that the One who calmed the storm in scripture is still alive and well; we are living proof! We believe with everything within us that if He would do it for us, He will do it for you.

[KJ] One of my favorite youth pastors, Jeanne Mayo, led me to this title, "Affair-Proofing Your Marriage." What a great thing to do! We spend so much effort and preparation in so many other areas of our lives, why is it that we don't take the same preparation and effort when dealing with our marriages? We winterize our homes to prepare for freezing conditions in anticipation of seasonal storms, and we may search the Internet extensively in hopes of finding the right car. What if we used that same diligence and detail to make our marriages successful? Ever heard the old saying, "Where your heart is, there your treasure will be also"? Well, we also believe that, "Where our time is, our treasure will be also." This means whatever we place or invest value in is where we will spend most of our time.

As a society, we often value material things more than the most important relationship we have next to God. We major on the minor and spend countless lifetime moments engaged in purposeless pursuits. We have the power to change that, but first we must prepare ourselves and acknowledge some critical facts about marriage. If we know the facts and we know what is at stake, we will know better how to prepare to win. For all our sports fanatics, this would be the equivalent of studying films of your opponent in order to know how to win the championship.

Readings from *The Normal Bar* by Northrup, Schwartz, and Witte in 2013 researches that statistically 66.6% of men will have an affair during the course of a marriage, and nearly 50% of women will have an affair during the course of a marriage. This statistic[8] is staggering! Unfortunately, *the statistics for Christian marriages are no different than those for non-Christians.* Studies also tell us that 36% of affairs begin with a co-worker (typically on a business trip), 17% begin with a brother or sister-in-law, and 21% (for men) and 32% (for women) happen with an old flame or perhaps with a friend's spouse. 45% of men and women have admitted being attracted to their spouse's friends. *71% of all affairs are with someone with whom the spouse is associated.* A significant number of all affairs are now somehow related to social media. All of these statistics are not meant for paranoia but to remind us all that these are issues we need to take seriously. We need to set up good, healthy boundaries that will ensure our success in navigating these relationships and avoiding adding to the statistics.

Additional studies[9] researched at Infidelityfacts.com further submit that many affairs stem from an unmet emotional or physical need. The information submitted there suggests that men and women are hardwired differently, so the reasons why women and men cheat are fundamentally different. We determined previously that men are visual creatures by nature, so often the most common reason for a man to become unfaithful is attraction plus an unmet physical need. Women, on the other hand, are more audible. Therefore, infidelity is usually sourced by an unmet emotional need. She usually enters into an affair trying to fill some kind of emotional void she is not receiving from her spouse; she seeks someone who will make her feel loved, understood, cared for and heard.

So, in our preparation to win at this thing called marriage, let's review some truths. The truth is that there are often many different reasons why men and women become unfaithful to their spouses. A September 2013 article from Examiner.com gives great insight into the *Top 10 Reasons Men and Women Cheat* ([10]www.examiner.com)

We have taken this list and compiled it with counseling experiences to create our own Top 12 List of Why Men & Women Have Affairs. These are a list of reasons (not excuses) that have become realities for many who have experienced an affair. This list is tremendously more extensive, yet we just cited the more popular and recurrent responses.

12 Truths Why Men Have Affairs

1. Feels Unappreciated or Undervalued: The need to be needed

2. Lack of Communication and Emotionally Dissatisfied

3. Thrill: Infatuation, desire to experiment outside of the marriage, variety

4. Flesh: It was only physical; she didn't mean anything to me

5. Growing Apart: Wife has changed, nags me or doesn't seem to get me

6. Ego: Prove manhood due to low moral values and self-esteem

7. Drugs, Alcohol or Peer Pressure

8. Weakness: Can't say no

9. Secret: She'll never find out

10. Addiction

11. Revenge

12. To End the Marriage: Wanted an excuse to divorce

1. Truths Why Women Have Affairs

1. Lack of Emotional Intimacy: Seeks emotional connection/ emotionally starved

2. Loneliness

3. Revenge: He cheated first, or she wanted to make him jealous

4. Boredom

5. Feeling Trapped

6. Lack of Sex, Intimacy and Romance: Sexually deprived

7. Affirmation: The man made her feel undesirable; she feels he doesn't find her sexy

8. Adventure: Infatuation to feel "alive" again; seeks excitement

9. Low Self Esteem, Undervalued

10. Anger

11. Fraternal: Marriage feels more like friends than lovers after time

12. To End the Marriage: Wanted an excuse to divorce

Listed above are the earthly *symptoms* that often lead to unfaithfulness in marriage. We would like to journey deeper beyond the symptoms and explore the spiritual *problems* that exist that cause these issues in the first place. We will now provide nine spiritual reasons spouses become unfaithful to their spouse.

9 *Spiritual* Truths Behind Affairs

1. The Sinful, Human Nature of Man

[MJ] A true or somewhat accurate statistic in Christian marriages is far more difficult to determine because this topic is probably one of the more taboo subjects that people are reluctant or unwilling to talk about, especially in the church. Many couples are embarrassed, ashamed or guilty as they remain trapped within the sinful world of adultery. We believe it is the unwillingness to talk about this topic, especially within ministries across the nation, that keeps so many people bound; secrecy sets others up for failure when information to affair-proof our marriages is withheld. There are no guarantees in life, but one thing is certain; if we don't prepare, we are preparing to fail.

No one had to teach us how to sin. When our daughter Samantha was two, there was no shortage in her finding the things she should not touch and creating mischievous opportunities. We often would find ourselves training her in what was right as opposed to what was wrong. Sin is natural, as we are born into this world as sinners in need of God's mercy and saving grace. If we may come to this realization, it opens the revelation that we also may be saved by his grace.

2. Hunger, Rebellion & Pleasure

[KJ] As I speak both from research and personal experience, most adultery begins with some sort of hunger. Whether it is a hunger for affection, time, attention, sex, affirmation, respect or security, a hunger gone unchecked can turn into an uncontrollable, insatiable appetite that needs to be addressed quickly before it seeks to become satisfied outside of the marriage. I have personally found that the pleasure of sin is but for a moment, yet the devastating results of that moment can last a lifetime.

Women are more subject to emotional affairs than men. This commonly occurs when she has confided in someone matters of a sensitive nature and there is a bond of trust with that person. This often stems from the need to be listened to. This may happen to men as well who become emotionally dissatisfied, opening an access outside of the marriage to someone who is a friendly listening ear, a shoulder to cry on or someone who understands that your spouse, "Just doesn't understand,"

We must seek to renew our minds daily. What we think, we become. Adorning our head with the helmet of salvation is crucial, an essential garment for this battle. Football players are not just encouraged to wear their helmets, but required. All sin begins with a thought, and that thought is planted by someone or something. Catching our thoughts early is the key. Incubated thoughts grow quickly and they need to be uprooted, not buried and watered. 2 Corinthians 2:5 instructs us to *"cast down every vain imagination that tries to exalt itself against the knowledge of God and bring into captivity every thought to the obedience of Christ."*

Rebellion refers to knowing right from wrong yet choosing the latter, in defiance of God's plan for righteousness. The entire chapter of Romans 7 deals with the struggle of man knowing that when we desire to do good, evil is always present. It speaks of how the mind desires the things that are holy, yet the flesh desires unrighteousness. Because we know that the body must do whatever the mind tells it to do, the advantage is that if we renew our minds daily, our flesh must submit to what we mediate and think on. We cannot live our lives as though there is no expiration date.

The reality is that sin can be pleasurable. However, there is a cost or wage that must be paid in exchange for receiving the feelings derived from our unrighteous encounters. Sin can be fun and even enjoyable, yet the feeling is temporary and ultimately, sooner or later, leads to guilt, shame, condemnation and finally, death. The one who originated "Y.O.L.O. (you only live once)" was a liar. Actually, the full-length feature lasts for all eternity and only begins once we have completed this trailer, this life. The trailer is short. As we reflect on our lives in this theatrical fashion, what will your personal reviews look like, based on this lifetime? Blockbuster or lackluster?

3. Identity Crisis

Lack of or low self-esteem is often a direct reflection of not knowing who we are in Christ. If the issue is not identified and affirmation not supplied by the spouse and then confirmed by the Spirit, men and women might seek affirmation and value from others. One example of where the symptoms of this issue may surface is on our jobs.

Today, more women and men are working together and spending time outside of their homes, and consequently, workplace relationships develop. Spending inappropriate time with coworkers can put us in compromising situations that could potentially harm or even replace the relationship we are supposed to have with our spouse. Pleasing people on the job, seeking affirmation from others outside of our spouse and entertaining seemingly harmless but curious interactions can land either party in a predicament that is unhealthy in a marriage.

4. Social Media

[MJ] Modern day and evolving technology that provides resources like Facebook, Instagram, Twitter, Snap Chat, Pinterest, etc. have dramatically changed the way we interact with the world, both past and present. Nowadays, our cell phones are rarely used for actual conversation, and the "selfie" glamorizes our desire to be seen. Our office mainframes evolved into laptops that now have trespassed beyond the home workspace and have infiltrated our bedrooms. This effortless accessibility at the stroke of a key provides greater access to people from our past (ex: boyfriends, girlfriends and unhealthy relationships).

While writing this, current online statistics[11] gathered from a Huffington Post.com article from 2012 correlated that 20% of all divorces in America were directly related to Facebook. Access to those old flames do more than cause a few sparks; fanning those embers can create wildfires that consume everything in their paths, including children and material possessions, not to mention our hearts. The challenge here is that one doesn't even have to search for these opportunities, as they often find us. The enemy is roaming like a lion *seeking* whom he may destroy. We don't always have to look for trouble; many times it will find us. If we aren't deeply hidden in Christ, we are extremely accessible and easy to find.

5. Unresolved Conflict

[KJ] In chapter 11, we talked about not leaving conflict unresolved before going to bed each evening. In adhering to this principle, we are able to potentially shut this door. It is important to not let things fester or go without resolution for long. If we're offended, we should speak it; if we're hurt, we should express it and if we are lacking something, it is important to share it. Unresolved conflict creates a breeding ground for infidelity and plants seeds of unforgiveness, yielding the fruit of revenge. Some may be thinking, "This could never happen to me." These are often famous last words or words included in the documents for divorce. It wouldn't hurt to have conversations with our spouses about these issues to safeguard our marriages, against even the most distant of possibilities. Miscommunication or the lack thereof is a part of the problem that leads directly to the infidelity solutions spouses often choose.

6. Impurity

[MJ] Hidden sin, addictions, pornography, masturbation, fetishes, childhood abuse and many other countless unchecked sources of impurities in our lives at some point become a reality. What's hidden on the inside ultimately reveals itself on the outside. Releasing our weaknesses into the open makes sin less likely to unexpectedly *sneak up on us*. If we are on guard, it is less likely for the enemy's tactics to be effective in our marriages.

7. Spiritual Death

[KJ] This is where boredom, monotony and routine are birthed. Most affairs initiated and experienced by men happen to be physical in nature, while for women they are initiated by forming emotional bonds prior to becoming physical. Interesting that Infidelity. com also mentions that most affairs initiated by women typically last three times longer than those initiated by men.[12] Men often fall because of a physical need or desire; this can be fueled by a need for sex, lack of adventure, lack of attraction or ego. Falling into lackluster habits, uninspired communication or romance, and lack of physical intimacy for him and emotional/verbal intimacy and stimulation for her are all warning signs that the street we are on could lead to a dead end. When we are spiritually alive in Christ, it is nearly impossible to be dead in the world. We become dead *to* the world (our flesh) but not in it (our spirit). When couples are growing in the word together, falling deeper in love with Jesus manifests in marriage by falling deeper in love with our spouses.

8. Pride

[MJ] One of the biggest mistakes any man or woman can make is believing they are beyond the capability to fall into this trap. Pride creates a false reflection of ourselves that has us believe we are stronger than we actually are. "That would never happen to me," and "I never even have thoughts like that" can lead to "It's harmless, we're just friends," and finally to "How did this ever happen to me?" Underestimating the enemy is overestimating our ability to humanly fight a spiritual battle. *Pride comes before the fall* for a reason. There is a sobering clarity on the other side of pride. Pride blurs reality.

9. Fantasy

[MJ] Communication with our spouses to share and express desires provides an outlet to often fulfill each other in marriage. When these thoughts are internalized and go unexpressed, curiosity, infatuation and sexual appetite grow hungry when the desires could be satisfied within the marriage. Many men who have affairs still love their wives and have no desire for divorce. I have personal testimony that my infidelity wasn't to harm my wife but to supplement needs I felt I could not communicate to her. There was not a readiness or willingness for me to share my weakness with her. I loved her, yet there was a war raging within. This ancient proverb somewhat describes my personal experience.

Two Wolves:

A Cherokee Legend

An old Cherokee was teaching his grandson about life. "A fight is going on inside me," he said to the boy.

"It is a terrible fight and it is between two wolves. One is evil - he is anger, envy, sorrow, regret, greed, arrogance, self-pity, guilt, resentment, inferiority, lies, false pride, superiority, and ego." He continued, "The other is good - he is joy, peace, love, hope, serenity, humility, kindness, benevolence, empathy, generosity, truth, compassion, and faith. The same fight is going on inside you - and inside every other person, too."

The grandson thought about it for a minute and then asked his grandfather, "Which wolf will win?"

The old Cherokee simply replied, "The one you feed."

I love this story and how it simply outlays the fact that what we feed will grow. If we are entertaining external unrighteous thoughts, they infiltrate our body and mind, and ultimately, begin to influence our heart. Pastor Dennis Rouse simply shares that we are spirits, who have a mind and we live in a body. The war between flesh and spirit is either won or lost in our mind.

> *The flesh lusts against the Spirit, and the Spirit against the flesh; and these are contrary the one to the other; so that ye cannot do the things that ye would. Galatians 5:17 (KJV)*

In personal testimony, I was feeding my flesh and body with food and lust rather than my spirit and soul with the word and righteousness. I found myself time and time again in a losing battle against an enemy I was ill-equipped to fight. I couldn't use "the devil made me do it" as an excuse either. This time, my enemy was my "inner-me." I was engaged in battle; the devil was simply providing me with ammunition to wage war against myself.

Now we prepare to dive deep.

Kristin's Story

[KJ] We were married just under two years when the infidelity began. I had just had a baby, I was very invested in my company and was not very attentive to Montell and definitely not in tune with his needs. After all, I had a company to run. I had desires and career aspirations to achieve *outside of my husband.*

When I became pregnant with my first daughter, Montell began to travel. A lot. He was gone 352 days of year two in our marriage. So began the infidelity. I did love to travel, but after I got pregnant, I was not well enough to travel, and it was really rough on my body. I chose to stay home, but what I also unknowingly chose was to uncover my husband and leave him open to temptation. Of course women were readily available and willing to make their moves on him, but in my mind, I thought *we were above reproach (pride).* I had discussed with all of our employees the consequences that if they ever allowed any "funny business" to go down, they would be fired. I would shut it all down, meaning the entire business, which included their very livelihood. (For the record, ultimatums never work.) I left Montell out there by himself for weeks at a time. In retrospect, it now seems silly to me, but I just didn't know what I didn't know at the time. I was so focused on our business that I didn't pay attention to what was going on in our marriage. Our marriage was definitely not my priority. This caused us to be out of alignment, and it would lead down a pathway of infidelity. *This continued for years without me knowing.*

It wasn't until year seven that my world came crashing down on me. My best friend called and cancelled a trip we were scheduled to take together and asked to speak to my husband. She had found out about all the indiscretions, and she basically gave him an ultimatum, "You tell her or I will!" With that, my husband came clean, and I found out the last five years of our marriage was a farce. I hated every minute of it, as some of these women were my "friends."

While I had left for a few days to contemplate my course of action, everything within me wanted to leave the marriage for good. However, at the prompting of my best friend, she asked, "Have you prayed about this?"

My response to this was a resounding, "Absolutely *not*!" Somehow -- deep within my spirit beneath the pain, shame and emotions -- I already knew what His answer would be and quite frankly, I was not interested in hearing that! I knew that forgiving him and taking him back would cost me everything. My dignity, reputation, self-esteem and what little pride I felt I had left would be gone. I would have to lay my whole life down and resume a new one without any regard for the previous life; that was not an easy pill to swallow. However, the one thing I did know was that God knew more than I did. So after much lamenting, embarrassment and heartache, I laid my marriage at the altar and cried out to God, "Lord, what do you want from me? What do you want me to do?"

In an authoritative yet still small voice He said, *"Stay! You and your daughter's lives depend on it!"* Wow.

What do you do with information like that? Do you disregard it based on how you feel or do you rein in your thoughts and remind yourself that you serve a sovereign God that knows what you don't and trust Him? Here were the facts I was faced with:

1. I knew this was the husband God had chosen for me, so He must have known this was going to happen.
2. He knew what was to come, and I did not.
3. I definitely had no clue what to do other than to run a million miles an hour in the other direction.

In conclusion, I had to come to the resolve that I must trust God and believe what He said over what I said. I decided to stay, but if I am completely transparent, in the beginning, I only stayed for the sake of my daughter.

This is a critical impasse where many marriages end. We ask and God answers, yet we proceed to choose our own answers over His. We choose *my will* over *Thy will* be done. Our emotions cause us to abandon ship, our shame makes us throw in the towel and our pride leads us to abort the miracle God was prepared to birth. I stayed on the sinking ship holding the towel, with only the hope of knowing Jesus was with me on the boat.

As time passed and the memories became more distant, God began to do surgery on my husband. He resolved to change his behavior and heart, and I began to heal. Funny that as He changed my husband's heart, my heart began to heal! It was a long, hard road to healing, but I will tell you that it was worth every minute. Seeing the man he has now become in Christ, you would never believe what his past looked like. Montell is now an amazing, Godly, kind, loving, faithful and attentive man of God; everything I could have ever dreamed of and prayed for. God knew what I did not know! Thank God I trusted Him and not my own human, fleeting emotions.

I never would have had the opportunities I am afforded now. Not only do I get to see him walk in his calling, pray for the sick, be the spiritual head of our household, minister to people, be an amazing husband and great dad, but I also get the bonus of *the promise*. What's the promise? I now get to watch him worship with our daughter, the other life God told me that was depending on me staying. I also now have two sons and another daughter I would have never had without making that one choice. They (my children) are delightful and extreme joys in my life. God brought us through the fire and, through His grace and mercy, we don't have any remnants of the smoke. It would have been much easier to leave. I had a legal right to leave, but I had the spiritual mandate to stay.

My husband was in bondage, and Jesus set him free. God used me to help my husband get free. What was in darkness came to light. This allowed my fears as well (insecurities, childhood abuse, sexual inhibitions) to be brought to light and I, too, was set free. After all, in marriage we were one; it was impossible for him to remain in bondage and for me not to feel the chains. We were both set free.

God had so much more for me. Thank the Lord I didn't settle for what I had for me, as it absolutely paled in comparison. I could have divorced. I could have ¼ the children, see them ½ the time and received ½ the finances from a separation settlement. I believe what Christ did in our marriage reminds us, "Why settle for ½ or when My desire is to give you *all*?" God knew exactly what I needed and how He could get my husband there. Somehow, only through the power of Jesus, I was able to forgive him. He then used my forgiveness to love my husband back to Christ and into his rightful place with God. We serve a redemptive and kind Father who always meets us where we are and walks with us every step of the way. He is a good father.

I have shared from my personal story what happened in our relationship, but I came across a book by Peggy Vaughn that she wrote about affairs, called "The Monogamy Myth."[13] This book would have been extremely helpful early on in my marriage, and could have helped to relieve some of the heartache and pain. In her book, she describes three main causes of affairs. First, there are factors that *push* people into an unhealthy relationship (like problems, faults, individual or relationship shortcomings), factors that *pull* people into unhealthy relationships (like excitement, curiosity, enhanced self-image or "falling in love"), and finally, there are societal factors that *contribute* to affairs (such as the media selling sex, lack of honesty with teens about sexual issues and the secrecy surrounding unfaithfulness, in general).

So much of what I read resonated with what I felt caused the unfaithfulness in our marriage. We had issues in our marriage because our marriage was out of alignment with the will of God for our lives. I was more comfortable with my role as CEO than wife; I lost focus on what was important to my husband physically, emotionally and spiritually. He was pulled into an affair because it was exciting; surely he felt his self-image being enhanced since I clearly wasn't giving him the time or attention he needed. How could I give him the time and attention he deserved when we had a to-do list a mile long? I'm sure curiosity played a role in it, to see if he could get away with it. Not to mention the industry we were in frowned upon marriage and children. I was looked upon as weak or less than because of being married and having children. We had been using sex to sell records and even sang about some of these adulteress topics in our songs. This was a recipe for disaster, but in reality, we didn't know what we didn't know. Again, that's why

God said, "My people are destroyed because of lack of knowledge." It is my prayer as you read this content that you read it, absorb it, talk about it and apply it to your life.

Montell's Story

[MJ] I was dysfunctional in marriage long before I was married. Childhood access to *Penthouse, Hustler* and *Playboy* Magazines gave me unhealthy glimpses into pornographic templates I believed were supposed to be normal expectations in sexuality. The descriptive words used also created visuals of how I perceived sexual needs were to be communicated in my future relationships. Add to this that I lost my virginity at age 19 outside of marriage and continued sexual activity through most of my college and fraternity life and what results is a fertile, negative breeding ground for defective, intimate seeds to take root.

Upon laying eyes on Kristin for the very first time, something within me *knew* she would be my wife. Even in all my sin and dysfunction, I still had been asking God to provide the woman He had for me to become my wife. This was never a question I had to ask myself or revisit.

In the beginning, Kristin and I were a great business together. Our marriage was more of a formality we both chose in order to ward off the "evils" of the big, bad music industry that we heard would consume us if we weren't married prior to entering. In retrospect, there was a lot of truth in what we were being told, yet we had no married mentors in the business to help us navigate *why we did what we did*. We just knew it was the thing to do to sustain us before taking the ride.

Early on, traveling together was a blast. The tricky part was being a somewhat normal, married couple in private, and then in public, pretending that we were *not together*. To make this believable, I would have to compromise myself to allow women into the space where my wife would normally stand. I remember being on the set of *This is How We Do It* and a girl who was hired to be the "object of my attention" was seated next to me. She touched my face and made sensual advances for the camera. It was what was supposed to happen, yet inside me I heard non-stop conflicting spiritual warnings were firing off between my flesh and my spirit. This was only the beginning. Years of compromise, songs, videos and career over marriage would allow God's *still small voice* to become softer and softer as the world called out to me at an almost deafening volume.

I always had a choice. God always provided me with a way of escape, but to say there was a barrage of women and alcohol available to me at every turn was an understatement. The presence of these things were there both when my wife was absent as well as when she was right there beside me. The enemy is bold like a lion, seeking whom he may destroy. Sadly, there were times when my wife would be with me and she would retire to our hotel room to bed, while the remaining crew members and I would go out to clubs and entertain for the purpose of "feeding the fame" and keeping up the appearances of my celebrity status.

Marriage was not our priority and the blueprint for us did not exist. I was unaware the satisfaction I was seeking from intimacy with my wife would have to first be satisfied by me having an intimate relationship with God. My intimacy with God was surface, at best. This also reflected in my intimacy with my wife. How else could I have not known my wife and I never experienced orgasm (us together or her alone) until seven years into our marriage? It's because my only reference was from dysfunctional experiences. A lap dance or masturbation was the only surface frame of reference I had. Many intimate years were lost during this season of our lives.

I often felt alone, even while being surrounded by thousands of people. I would manufacture moments of intimacy to fill voids of loneliness. Playing cards, Monopoly, watching movies and insulating myself with people rather than God or His word would only fight off the world's external advances for so long. At some point, the sinful advances would become internal, and I would have very little refuge from fleshly overload from all angles.

Years of this bondage contained more forgotten names, cities, near misses and moral failures than I care to recollect. It was all hidden, yet God knew every fall I had taken, and somehow, He knew the conflict I was experiencing within meant that He still had me. To this day, I can't understand how He would still consider me to be His, even after my failures in marriage. The most ridiculous yet beautiful thing about God is that He could somehow take the worst of the worst (me) and still use my story for His plan of redemption for *you*. I lived a life of guilt and shame. I was guilty about what I had done; I was ashamed about what I had become. It wasn't until my sin was exposed that I was faced with the most important decision of my life, next to accepting Christ as my Savior: "Do you want to save your marriage?" I truly believe that had I not been able to answer in the affirmative and forsake all that had me enslaved to sin, the Lord may have told Kristin to leave instead of stay.

I confessed my sins to God to be forgiven but to be honest, that wasn't *how I got healed. "Confess your sins, one to another, and pray for each other so that you may be healed," (James 5:16, NLT).* This was the plan for God to heal me. He used my wife, my marriage, her shoulder, her ears and her heart to absorb every damaging detail I could recollect from every hidden sin and escapade so that the enemy could no longer have a hold of me. She got a small glimpse of what carrying the cross may have been like for Christ as the things I shared with her were seemingly unbearable. Yet as she carried it, He carried her. I was healed in my confession. Porn addiction, masturbation, soul ties. Everything I had done in darkness was brought to light.

Had the Lord not prepared her to endure what was to come, I would not have gotten free and neither would she. Whether you are the husband or the wife who is currently secretly harboring unconfessed sins that have you living in guilt and shame, I assure you that you are merely existing, *not living*. Keep in mind that within the covenant of marriage, if your spouse is bound, you are bound.

The enemy will have you believe you would rather take a secret to the grave rather than hurt your spouse. The reality is that harboring the secret keeps the enemy from being exposed as the liar that he is and doesn't allow the light of the world to consume the darkness of your life!

Do you want to be free?

Do you want your spouse to be free?

Do you want to be forgiven?

Do you believe you have the ability to forgive the unforgivable?

If you don't, do you know that in our weakness He is made strong?

Do you need to confess?

Do you want to be healed?

Please take a moment from reading the questions and actually answer them. Just as you inherit the genes of your parents and learn from the behaviors of those whom you observe, your spirit inherits everything that your physical body does. You can't take money, fame or anything physical with you after you die but your spirit inherits the attitudes, tendencies, character and mentality with which your body lived. In religious terms, your spirit will have either sins or righteousness, depending on how you chose to live your life. How you live your physical life will determine your spiritual fate.

How to Protect Your Marriage against Affairs

[MJ & KJ] There are some very practical methods we can implement to guard our sacred covenant against the possibility of an affair. Hosea 4:6 shares that, "My people are destroyed because of lack of knowledge." Many people don't start looking to see if there is a hole in the boat until it begins sinking. We suggest having a plan and being prepared rather than to get side swiped and try and recover from it. Our chances of success increase as we prepare. We are not suggesting we plan for an affair; we are suggesting we plan to guard against attacks of infidelity that may arise to jeopardize our marriages. Research[14] reveals that the likelihood of having to deal with infidelity in a marriage is more than one of every two. This means half of all marriages will possibly encounter an adulterous affair in some form or another. Sadly, it's possible that statistics may be even higher because those numbers are only based on people who've actually admitted to having an affair. Many affairs occur and continue without being detected or confessed.

No matter how good we are and how faithful we believe our spouse is, we all have a real enemy. This enemy can cause even the strongest men and women with the purest of intentions to fall, or at least become compromised, with the possibility and opportunity to wander outside of the marriage. The possibility is real. So let's discuss why infidelity is on the rise and more common than we may have previously thought.

The Line in the Concrete

Many couples draw a line in the sand only to realize that when the waves of life rise and fall over that soft sand, the line can sometimes be erased, removed and redrawn. Some things simply must be etched in stone. For the sake of our marriages, here are a few examples of boundaries we have set:

1. No riding alone in a car with someone of the opposite sex alone, *no matter who they are*. No spending excessive time with anyone outside of our spouse.

2. Always have a third party present when having a meeting with someone of the opposite sex. When a closed door is required have accountability, notify someone and make sure the office is windowed.

3. When interacting with a spouse's friends, it should be when spouses are together, and men should contact men and women should contact women. Plans should be made with the wives by the wives or with the husbands by the husbands. I do not contact my husband's friends without first telling him in advance and detailing the intent and conversation, and via versa. This is why having mutual friends

is advised. We don't access our spouse's friends without advance notice and purpose for the contact.

4. No business trips with anyone of the opposite sex alone. I will accompany my husband or another trusted accountable male will go.

5. No lunch or dining plans with the opposite sex without a third party present, preferably your spouse. Getting defensive when asked about time spent outside of the marriage could be a warning sign that unhealthy behaviors are present.

6. Have an itinerary to account for whereabouts. Establishing trust is far easier than rebuilding it once it is broken. Develop a pattern of transparency to account for daily and nightly activities when possible and time spent before it ever happens. Call when changes come up. This may seem extreme or excessive, yet we lived an extreme and excessive lifestyle that brought about extreme and excessive warfare to overtake our marriage. Others may not need all these safeguards. We implemented these actions in efforts to save our marriage and were able to withstand the onslaught of the enemy where others who didn't take these measures have thrown in the towel.

7. Allow our spouse full access to all social media sites, and provide passwords for accountability to make sure nothing ever remains unchecked or hidden. This is not license for

the insecure spouse to snoop through cell phone and emails; these are measures for those rooted in Christ and trusting in His blueprint for faithfulness in marriage to institute for a peace and security only found in His architecture.

8. When someone from the past comes into the present, no matter whom or how, we immediately talk about it, just to make sure everything is always beyond reproach. It's better to bring it up rather than a spouse to find out, become insecure and ask about it. Unspoken concerns about personal appearance before seeing someone outside of the marriage may also be something to consider, as this is a sign that an emotional affair may be present, even subconsciously.

[KJ] In addition to the previously mentioned suggested boundaries, it is also wise to be mindful that there are certain seasons of our marriage when we should heighten our alert to guard against these tendencies of monotony and routine. Not adjusting after the first year, focus changes, having a child or children, experiencing a sickness or injury, financial hardship and all of these instances can lead to a spouse being emotionally or physically unavailable in the marriage.

Here are a few suggestions to guard against becoming martially complacent, or in a "place of compromise," within the marriage:

1. Keep guards up between years five and seven when achievements and goals originally set in the beginning of your marriage are met or missed.

2. Reset, refocus and readjust new goals together.

3. Keep intimacy frequent, intentional, & interesting. Spice is nice!

4. Consistently maintain a date night. When midlife calls and the kids are going off to college and the season of life and responsibilities are shifting, secure the communication and the intimacy connection so that you actually know each other when you get to this juncture in life. So many couples raise families, work careers and reach the end of those seasons only to realize they never invested in knowing their spouse. It is important to create new goals, common interests and plans regularly so that as this season comes we are still in one accord and not searching for a new identity.

Clearly, this is not an all-inclusive list; however, it is a start so that you can begin setting up or adding to some healthy boundaries to establish a firm and solid blueprint. In regards to helping our husbands create healthy boundaries; I have the firm belief that the best defense against affair-proofing your marriage is a good sexual offense. People who are extremely satisfied in their sex lives are a lot less likely to act on outside attractions. Most men who are sexually satisfied within their marriages are way less likely to be attracted to outside distractions.

When trying to affair-proof your marriage, be aware that no one is exempt from having an affair and make a commitment to honesty. Next, you must maintain open communication with each other; this is an ongoing exercise. That means being honest about everything that impacts your marriage, even attraction or encounters with people from your past or attractions to others. You must leave the things that have happened behind and not pack a bag and bring it along for the ride, only to be unpacked and hurled at your spouse during times of conflict. If you are going to forgive and move on, do it! Leave those bags at the foot of the cross and cover them in the blood of Jesus.

Recovery

[MJ & KJ] What if you've already been down this road and are on your way to recovery? How can we rebuild our marriages?

First of all, we have to make each move a matter of prayer, remembering our thoughts are not like God's. His thoughts will serve to be more useful and accurate. When we are actively praying for God to bless someone, it is much harder to remain angry with him or her. We need to let go so that forgiveness can kick in and bitterness fade away. This is easier said than done, yet we can do all things through Christ Jesus that gives us strength. Chances are, on our own we will *not* be able to overcome and recover from the aftermath of an affair. *The only true way to avert crisis is to revert to Christ-is.*

Secondly, it is important to answer all questions that are looming around the incident and begin building trust through actions and not just words; words at this juncture are cheap. Just like faith without works is dead, words and sentiments without action become useless.

Thirdly, you must cut off all contact(s) with the third party completely. Disengage immediately. If it is a job, relationship, friendship or anything else that pushes us toward feeling anything beyond our affections for our spouse, we advise quitting, fleeing or running *immediately*. Trust cannot be properly reestablished between spouses if communication with the third party is still open and available. So we repeat: If that person is on your job, it's time to start looking for a new job. *Compromise is not an option.* There will never be a peace for your spouse (or for yourself) as long as that door remains open.

Fourthly, you must make a commitment to be honest in your communication and engage in frequent "check-in" talks to make sure you are both on the same page. This means establishing accountability with your spouse and possibly other ministry or wise counsel persons who may walk alongside you to assist in rebuilding trust in the marriage. We always do better when someone is watching. There are many other ways to restore a marriage following an affair, yet these are critical steps on your way to healing and restoration.

Most importantly, the realization of Christ's love, mercy, grace and forgiveness extended to us as individuals is the secret to finding the ability to extend love, mercy, grace and forgiveness to a spouse who has been unfaithful. Forgiveness eliminates the enemy's ability to torment us. After an affair, we can become bitter or better. We can decide to become victims or victors. Exchange denial and escape for freedom and liberation. True transformation happens from the inside out, so this process is not easy, nor is it quick. There is hope in Jesus, and in addition to that hope in the spirit, we are living examples and a testimony that there is also hope in the natural.

Our marriage is awesome, and we have experienced far more than we have shared in this book. Take the unfailing promises of God and our first 20 years of marriage and use them as a blueprint for your marital design where it applies. Our examples may or may not be relevant to your particular set of circumstances, but His plan applies everywhere. As all our marriages are designed to be built upon a solid foundation, you will be able to use the blueprint as you and your spouse begin or continue your own life together. Building takes time; rebuilding may take more time as together, we must determine if the foundation is solid enough to begin building again.

This will not happen overnight. This process takes time. No different than a fractured leg in a cast, it takes time to set, heal and begin rehabbing it to its original state. Keep in mind that in order for this to become a success story, you cannot allow yourself to go through the mental trickery, or play the blame game. You have to create some healthy boundaries to affair-proof your marriage moving forward. Even when it doesn't feel like you can, you can do it. It will be worth it and it can be totally healed, redeemed and restored. We are living witnesses. *If* God would do it for us through the power of Jesus, He will do it for anyone who believes. The good news for you is that He *did* do it for us. *This is how He does it.*

This is how we do it. – Montell & Kristin Jordan

Endnotes

Sources and resources used in research:

i www.census.gov

ii http://www.merriam-webster.com/dictionary/favor

iii www.theactionbible.com

iv http://www.merriam-webster.com/dictionary/marriage

v www.abcnews.com http://abcnews.go.com/GMA/HealthyLiving/divorce-contagious/story?id=11198347

vi According to psychologist Albert Mehrabian, http://center-for-nonverbal-studies.org/nvcom.htm

vii www.5lovelanguages.com

viii ˣExcerpted from the book THE NORMAL BAR. Copyright © 2013 by Chrisanna Northrup, Pepper Schwartz, and James Witte. Published by Harmony, an Imprint of the Crown Publishing Group, a division of Random House, Inc. **The Normal Bar** is the world's most extensive survey on romantic relationships, polling over 100,000 people and collecting over 1 million data points. The survey was conducted in 2011 using a powerful interactive survey tool called OnQ with the help of media partners The Huffington Post, Reader's Digest, AARP, iVillage, & AOL

[ix] www.infidelityfacts.com www.marriagehelpadvisor.com/2013/05/01cheating-myths-and-facts/ The Monogamy myth by Peggy Vaughn and excerpts from Smart Marriages Conference (Washington, DC , 1999)

[x] November 6, 2010 Examiner.com

[xi] http://www.huffingtonpost.com/2012/06/02/facebook-divorce-ipo-money_n_1541040.html

[xii] www.infideltyfacts.com

[xiii] The Monogamy myth by Peggy Vaughn

Additional references used from an unpublished work called **Married Forever**, a Family Ministries resource used at Victory World Church written by Anthony and Phyllis Breech and used by permission.